Feels Like The First Time

A True
Love Story

Shawn Inmon

Feels Like The First Time
A True Love Story
By Shawn Inmon

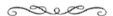

©2012 by Shawn Inmon

Cover Design/Interior Design: Linda Boulanger
www.TellTaleBookCovers.weebly.com

Published by Pertime Publishing

Also available in eBook publication

PRINTED IN THE UNITED STATES OF AMERICA

Dedication

*For Terri Lee, my sister and friend
on both sides of life's curtain.*

Steven D –
you're one of
my lifetime best
FRIENDS !

Prologue
February 10th, 1979

Dawn was at the side of the room, crying softly. I didn't want to see her tears, but I couldn't stop looking at her. I knew I might never see her again.

I needed to concentrate, but I couldn't focus. Maybe it was the fact that I hadn't slept in two days, or maybe I already knew how this was going to turn out. Either way, I couldn't follow what everyone was saying.

Dawn looked questioningly at her mom, who nodded her permission. She came and stood behind me, placing her hand on the back of my neck. When I felt her gentle touch, I couldn't hold my tears back anymore.

I realized it was quiet and everyone was looking at me. I took the wad of bills out of my jeans pocket and laid it on the table.

"I know you've told me I can never see Dawn again, but I can't agree to that. I'll agree not to see her for three years, but she'll be eighteen then and she can see me if she wants."

"Fine," Colleen said, eyeing me with contempt. It was clear she wasn't worried about Dawn wanting to see me in the future.

"That's it then," I said softly, almost to myself. There was nothing left to say. My composure was completely gone. Hot tears ran down my face, but I didn't care. This was the moment I had done everything to both cause and avoid. It was possible I might see Dawn again at some future date, but I would never see this Dawn. She was so lovely it broke my heart to look at her.

I went to her and put my hands on her shoulders. I looked deeply into her eyes. I didn't ask her to wait for me. I was trying to set her free.

"When we can see each other again, if you still love me, I'll be there for you. I promise I'll love you just the same."

She nodded. Her tears streamed down her face and she looked away.

I walked out of her house, across the familiar yard and into the rest of my life.

Where True Love Goes
December 1st, 2006

It had already been a very long day, but I wasn't in any hurry to get home to Enumclaw. As I drove north on I-5, I turned the volume up on the CD I had just bought that day–Yusuf Islam's *An Other Cup*.

I was exhausted and unhappy, but that was normal. At 46, I was slowly killing myself by eating too much, not exercising at all, and withdrawing from everyone around me. I didn't much care if I lived or died.

I had been in my second marriage for five years, but it felt more like a prison than a marriage. The divorce I knew was coming was just another in a long string of failed relationships stretching back thirty years.

Four years earlier, I had told my wife, Adinah, that I didn't love her.

"You don't get to do this," she replied. "If you think it changes anything, it doesn't."

And so life went on. I had tried to end our marriage ever since, with no success. I couldn't find the emotional strength to get it over with and say the magic words: *I want a divorce.*

I was still ninety minutes from Enumclaw and realized I was starving when I saw the last Centralia exit in my headlights. I jerked the wheel to the right at the last moment and cut off a gold sedan. I could barely hear the honk of their horn over my music, but I saw the finger, telling me to have a nice day.

I wasn't sure what food I might find on this exit, but when I pulled off the freeway, I instinctively turned left.

Up ahead, I saw a sign that read *Bill & Bea's*. I hadn't even known that place was still open. I'd eaten there a lot when I was in high school in the '70s but hadn't been back since I'd moved out of Lewis County.

Without a thought, I eased into the parking lot and got in line behind an old pickup truck. Yusuf Islam–the former Cat Stevens–was singing that he went where his true love goes. I clicked it off because I didn't particularly feel like listening to that sweet sentiment.

I was beginning to think the folks in the truck in front of me were never going to get their order when they finally pulled away, leaving a blue cloud of exhaust in their wake. I pulled ahead and waited to place my order. The girl at the drive-thru window smiled the way pretty young girls do at safe-looking older men. She took my order and disappeared.

A minute later another woman came to the window and asked me a question, but I didn't answer. An electric charge started at the top of my head and ran down my spine. My stomach flip-flopped and my hands went slick against the steering wheel.

I gaped at her. There was something about her, but I couldn't quite grab what it was. Just looking at her made my heart race. She had shoulder-length wavy auburn hair and soft features with brown eyes that jumped out at me. Her face swirled through my memory, but wouldn't come into focus.

"I just need to know if you want onions on your chicken sandwich," the woman repeated patiently.

I couldn't answer. My brain was stuffed with cotton.

"Yes, please," I finally mumbled. As she walked away, I thought maybe she felt something unusual too, but after a brief pause, she was gone.

Why were fireworks going off in my head? Who was that woman? She was attractive, but I see attractive women every day without acting like a fool. Through the drive-thru window, I could see her standing next to a flattop grill talking to the girl who had initially taken my order. The woman laughed suddenly and a thunderbolt hit me. I had never been able to forget those laughing brown eyes.

Dawn.

I hadn't seen her in twenty-seven years, but I knew it was her. I watched her slide gracefully between the counter and the grill to pick up an order. My mind wandered through long-buried memories I thought would never resurface.

She had lived for so long only as a memory; it was exhilarating to be this close to her again. As the years and decades passed, I came to believe I would never see her again. I accepted that, and even found odd comfort in the sense of closure. Finding her so unexpectedly sent my head spinning.

She brought the bag with my food. She took my money and handed me change with a tiny smile, but no hint of recognition. I wondered how she could not recognize me. She thanked me and turned away, but I couldn't let her vanish again.

"Did you go to Mossyrock High School?"

I took my foot off the brake and the car eased forward slightly.

"Yes."

"Class of '82?"

"No. '81."

Of course that was right. I was terrible at math under pressure. Her dark eyes focused intently through the drive-thru window. She put her hand on her hip and cocked her head slightly to the right, trying to place me.

"We went to school together."

She stared blankly, and I couldn't take the suspense. I gave her my biggest smile.

"Dawn, it's Shawn."

She was quiet for a moment.

"Shawn who?" she finally asked.

The question took all the air out of my ego. I wondered if I really looked so different. She examined me and I could tell she wasn't making the connection.

"Shawn Inmon. We lived next door to each other." I thought of adding, "You know... your first?"

She took a half-step back with stunned recognition. Her hands flew to her mouth and her brown eyes widened. It was a gesture the years never washed from my memory. I watched her expression flood with memories.

"Oh my God," she said. She paused and said it again. Each word was its own sentence. Oh. My. God. The young girl who took my order bounced over with a broad smile.

"Hi!" she said. "I'm Connie, Dawn's daughter."

I offered a lame smile to Connie. It was impossible for me to look away from Dawn. I laughed nervously but couldn't speak. Ten seconds of awkward silence followed while a Buick idled patiently behind me.

"I'm Shawn," I said weakly to Connie. My eyes were trained on Dawn. "Your Mom and I were friends a long time ago." Connie's smile told me she knew what kind of friends we had been. Dawn continued to murmur "oh, my, God" over and over, shaking her head. She chanted eerily, like a record needle stuck in a groove.

I tried to say something to break through, but I was so stunned at being this close to her, I couldn't think of anything worthwhile.

"It was good to see you," I mumbled. "I was just on my way home to Enumclaw". Dawn didn't seem to hear me. She was lost in her own world.

I grew frustrated at my inability to get my brain and tongue to work together. I turned to Connie.

"Tell your Mom it was good to see her, okay?" I gave her a poor attempt at a wink and failed. I took one last, long look at Dawn, and drove off, dizzy with the thought of her.

I wanted so badly to turn my car around and run into the tiny restaurant, yelling, "Dawn. Baby, it's me." I wanted to hold her tight against me and let the intervening years evaporate. Discretion and the ring on my finger prevailed, and I kept my wheels rolling forward, moving me further away from her with each second.

I had suppressed all thoughts of her for three decades. Now she was real again, and I couldn't prevent the surge of feelings. Memories, sensations, and emotions swept over me in relentless waves, choking me as I merged onto I-5.

The years had changed nothing. I loved her still, infinitely, after so much time. I loved her as I had when I kissed her tear-stained face goodbye on Valentine's Day, 1979.

I turned my music up and let the miles roll under my wheels. My body was in 2006, but my mind, spirit, and heart were firmly lodged in the 1970's.

A Long Time Ago

I was fifteen in the summer of 1975, trying to make the transition from childhood to whatever was next. Intellectually, I was mature beyond my years. Emotionally, I was way behind.

The OPEC oil embargo and energy shortage were fresh in everyone's mind. There was talk of saving energy for the first time. Daylight Savings Time lasted all year, and the national speed limit was lowered to 55 MPH to save gas. Gerald Ford was in the White House.

I lived in a 1965 doublewide trailer on a half-acre lot on the outskirts of Mossyrock, a flyspeck town in rural western Washington. The twin cities of Centralia and Chehalis sat forty miles away, with less than 30,000 people between them. When people said they were going "out town," that's what they meant.

I had already seen a lot of ups and downs in fifteen years. I spent my first five years living happily on a hundred-acre ranch with my Mom, Dad, brother, and three sisters. In the mid-'60s, the City of Tacoma dammed the river that ran through the Riffe Valley. That dam would eventually put our 100 acres underwater, so they took us to court and forced us to sell the ranch.

Dad found it hard to accept that the government could take the land he had painstakingly bought and farmed over a twenty-year period. Eventually, it took a toll on his health. On Halloween 1965, he had a heart attack and died. My three oldest sisters had already moved out and gotten married, so just my Mom, older brother Mick and I remained in our suddenly-quiet house.

Within a year, Mom met a man named Robert, one of the workers who had come to town to build the dam, and he stuck around. They were married in 1967 and I had a step-dad. By then my brother moved out and we moved into a trailer in Mossyrock. In two years, I had gone from living in a house filled with my family that sat on a hundred acres in an idyllic valley, to a doublewide on a cramped lot with my mom and a man that felt like a stranger.

My mom started drinking after my dad died. I didn't know much about alcoholism, but I figured she had a problem when I began finding Mason jars of vodka hidden around the house, including in my own dresser drawers.

Learning how to deal with her drinking was difficult enough, but the violence that came along with it made life scary and unpredictable for me. It didn't happen every day, but I came to realize that every few months there would be an explosion of anger between her and Robert. Next would come screaming, fist fights and the occasional trip to the ER. The first time it happened, I was sure that would be the end of things, and it would be back to just my mom and I on our own again. I was dismayed when everything was quickly forgotten. Over the years, these violent outbursts happened less frequently, but their impact never faded. They changed me forever.

I didn't adjust to all these changes well. I withdrew from into a self-made shell. I grew from an outgoing, happy five-year-old into a quiet, reserved teenager. I was gangly and awkward. I had grown more than ten inches in a single year, and I wasn't accustomed to my new body. I wore my hair however Mom told me to get it cut. My closet was full of T-shirts and bell-bottom pants, and I wore thick, black glasses that hadn't been in fashion since Buddy Holly's airplane went down in 1959. This goes a long way toward explaining why I had never had a date.

Most kids go through an awkward stage, and I was no

exception. Mine happened to last a little longer than most. I left behind the adorable cuteness of childhood at age nine, and didn't come into my own until I was eighteen. The years in between were an unrelenting stretch of homely awkwardness.

To make matters worse, one of my best friends and next door neighbor, Mark Panter, moved to Seattle. Mark and I had always found unique ways to stay busy. Several years before, my step-dad had brought home an old 100-gallon barrel. It leaned against our garden shed for a long time with water inside it and rust eventually formed. One day we tipped it over out of sheer boredom and it made a cool *shoosh-shoosh* sound, like a giant Indian rain stick.

During the summer of 1974, we spent hundreds of hours riding on top of the barrel, moving it along like competitive log rollers, and making up games that usually involved pitching each other headfirst onto the lawn. Our moms were sure we would kill ourselves, but it kept us out of the house, and more importantly, out of trouble.

If we could gather up a group of kids in the neighborhood, we'd turn the giant barrel on its end and use it as a base for a game of Werewolf. It was like Hide 'n Seek, except cooler—at least to us. Teenagers wouldn't be caught dead playing a kids' game today, but it was a different time. We didn't have iPods, cell phones or three hundred channels on TV.

At night Mark and I sat under the old cherry tree that grew in one corner of our yard and told stories and lies. We talked about girls we liked, and watched bats eating the moths hovering around the streetlight.

We heard that if you tossed a pebble into the path of a bat's sonar, it would follow it all the way to the ground and knock itself silly. For weeks we tried to make that happen without success, but the fun was in the trying.

One day that summer, Mark's dad lost his job and they moved away almost immediately. Watching bats eat moths was much less fun alone, and even if I could manage to sucker one into crashing into the ground, I didn't think anyone would believe me.

After a few weeks, I heard a new family was moving into Mark's place, but I wasn't hopeful. Their arrival reinforced the fact that my friend wasn't coming back. Plus, they were from California. In the mid-'70s, there were few things more unpopular in rural Washington than a transplanted Californian. There was a widely-held belief they had already used up everything good in California, and now they were invading our bucolic town to do the same.

The day the moving van arrived, Mom and my step-dad watched as everything was unloaded and carried inside. I was interested too, until I saw they didn't have any kids my age. After that I couldn't have cared less. Late that afternoon, our new neighbors emerged and walked around their new front yard, squinting in the sunlight. My step-dad was an outgoing type, and crossed the yard to say hello. I stayed behind in the driveway observing and pretending to work on my ten-speed bike. A large woman, Colleen wore a long, flowing muumuu. The man, Walt, was smaller and mostly kept to himself. Colleen seemed to control the conversation so that Walt may not have had a choice.

I recall Colleen saying how glad she was to be away from the urban sprawl of California. I heard her tell my step-dad about walking out of the house earlier and, seeing a plane flying overhead, shaking her fist at it and saying "How dare you, vestige of civilization, follow us to this cultural backwater."

And then it happened: the moment I first saw Dawn Adele Welch. She stepped out of the house quietly. When she heard her mom talking, she rolled her eyes, looked at me, turned on her heels, and went back inside.

Dawn was just a kid of eleven then. She was too young

for me to be interested in hanging out with her. But my first thought was, "that kid's got attitude." From a young age, she had the ability to let you know what she was thinking with very few words.

I rarely saw Dawn during the next few months. In addition to being four years older than her, I was a bookish boy who devoured Robert Heinlein and Edgar Rice Burroughs stories. Dawn loved her animals. She was always outside with her Dobermans, Peter and Chastity, her horse, Shiloh, and her goat named Fred.

Soon after Dawn moved in next door, school started and I began the daunting task of being a high school sophomore. I had suddenly grown to six feet tall and the basketball coach did a double-take as he passed me in the hall. In less than a year, I had gone from an under-sized guard to the tallest kid in my class. Unfortunately for the Mossyrock Vikings, I never grew another inch, and the added height only made me more awkward.

Dawn and I never saw each other at school. I was in high school, and she was at the junior high. We rode the #9 bus home, got off at the same stop, and walked quietly into our houses, but boredom would eventually force us outside. At that time there was no grudge fence between our houses, so it was natural to meet in the yard and talk quietly about school or friends. Because we lived on the outskirts of such a small town, there were few other kids around. I was so lacking for female conversation that I was happy to get some practice in, even if it was with the kid next door.

We slowly told each other the stories of our lives. Even at that age she was a series of interesting contradictions. She had an innate sense of calm. And yet, there was a wildness in her I was sure nothing could ever tame. She was shy and deliberate about trusting people. She could always make me laugh with a simple look. When I boasted about high school and my friends, her sidelong glance told me it was better to just be honest.

The best part of our friendship was the feeling that she accepted me for who I was: an older, nice kid who was safe to hang out with. I was clearly out of step with the cool crowd, but she didn't seem to care. She always accepted me for who I was, and that meant a lot.

Over time we became each other's fallback friend. If neither of us had another friend over, or didn't have practice of some sort, we would hang out. As the months passed, I started to look forward to hanging out with her. One evening we sat in our yard talking about things that were important to us–like whether Kojak was tougher than Baretta. That night Dawn told me her favorite song was *The Air That I Breathe* by The Hollies. Since she had told me that *Wildfire* by Michael Martin Murphy was her favorite song just a few weeks earlier, I pointed out she could only have one favorite song. She pointed out I was crazy, and she would have as many favorite songs as she wanted. That night, after Colleen called Dawn inside for dinner, I lingered outside, kicking the heads off of dandelions. I was sorry to see her go in, and I was a little surprised at the feelings for her that were growing inside me.

We never hung around each other when we were with our friends. That meant I never had to explain why I would be friends with a much younger girl, and she never had to explain why she hung out with such a nerd. But occasionally my two worlds collided.

One Friday night my friend Harold Crook came over after school to spend the night. We were planning to stay up and watch the creature feature hosted by The Count at midnight on Channel 7. The movies usually turned out to be big disappointments like *The Thing with Two Heads* and Channel 7 didn't even come in clearly on our television, but the idea of staying up until midnight to watch them was irresistible.

Harold Crook and I had been friends since kindergarten. He was the veterinarian's son and the kind of guy your parents wanted you to hang out with. He was earnest, intelligent, and he went to church because he liked it, not because his folks made him go. Like me, he had no experience with the fairer sex.

We had a few hours to kill between school and dinner that day, so we went outside and started tossing a Frisbee back and forth. Because we were nerds, we couldn't leave it at that. We created a set of rules, with points awarded and subtracted for difficult throws, angles, consecutive catches, and so forth. Soon we were trying to set new world records for Inmon Yard Frisbee.

Dawn's bedroom window looked onto our shared side yard. Midway through the game, Harold noticed Dawn standing behind her curtains, watching us. I was a little surprised she would watch something as boring as what Harold and I were doing.

At that moment, Harold tagged her with the nickname he called her forever. "I believe we have a Peeping Dawn," he said, attempting to be witty. Harold called her Peeping Dawn from that day on.

By early 1976, I was halfway through my sophomore year and I was starting to branch out and become my own person. Like most kids, my primary influences had been my parents. I grew up listening to whatever my parents were listening to: Nat King Cole, Herb Alpert & the Tijuana Brass, The Kingston Trio, or The Lettermen. I still loved that music, but I had acquired tastes my folks definitely didn't share. I had discovered Led Zeppelin, Pink Floyd and Bachman-Turner Overdrive, and my prized possession was my new *Frampton Comes Alive* double album.

For the first time I was beginning to think about the clothes I wore. I looked around the school to see what the popular kids were wearing, and thought about trying to dress the same way. I didn't have any money to buy those clothes but at least I was starting to be aware of the idea.

I was also making some decisions that would affect me for the rest of my life. I started going with Mom to her Alcoholics Anonymous meetings and learned that alcoholism can be inherited. That worried me a lot. I didn't want to go down the same awful path she was on. I decided that same day I was never going to drink. That decision stuck, and I still haven't had my first drink.

In February, Mom decided I could throw a birthday party, which surprised me. We never went hungry, but there was rarely money for extras like a birthday party. We rented the local hall, which was just a big empty room with a concrete floor and cinderblock walls. Since the place was big enough, Mom told me I could invite anybody I wanted.

On the day of the party, I took my record player and my small stack of albums and set it up in the hall. We set the cake on a small folding table and filled a garbage can full of ice and pop. We were ready to party like it was 1976.

I had a small difference of opinion with Mom about what lighting we would use during the party. She wanted the hall lit up like an interrogation room, and I was leaning toward complete darkness. We compromised by turning on the row of lights over the cake and pop, which left enough shadows to find a dark place to be alone with a special someone.

I invited Dawn and all the kids in my class. Nearly everyone showed up, and a lot of kids brought their own albums. The sound quality was what you would expect from concrete floors, cinderblock walls, and a cheap stereo, but nobody cared.

We danced for hours to the Steve Miller Band, Wild Cherry, Sweet, the Bee Gees and Earth Wind & Fire. Disco didn't suck in 1976, and if it did, we didn't care. We didn't see anything wrong with dancing to *Gimme Shelter* by the

Rolling Stones one minute, then doing *The Hustle* by Van McCoy the next.

Dawn was still in junior high, and most everyone else was in high school, so I tried to make sure she felt included. We danced together like teenagers did in the '70s–goofing off, laughing, and talking with friends more than dancing. As the party was winding down, I saw her standing off to the side of the room by herself. She had dressed up for the party. She wore black slacks and a nice jacket over a red long-sleeved top.

A fast song, *Rock'n Me* by the Steve Miller Band, was playing and that was a good one for a last dance with Dawn. I grabbed her arm and pulled her onto the dance floor. Just as that song began, a self-appointed DJ pulled the needle and dropped it again on the great '70's make-out song, *Stairway to Heaven* by Led Zeppelin. I was in a predicament. I'd already asked Dawn to dance, but I wouldn't have if I had known it was going to be a slow song. At the same time, I didn't want to insult her by saying she wasn't old enough to slow dance.

I acted like it wasn't a big deal and grabbed her hand and we danced the only way we knew how, huddled together, barely shuffling our feet. As Robert Plant wailed, Dawn put her arms around my neck and rested her head against my chest.

And that's when I felt something I never had before. I had no idea what it was, but I didn't want it to stop. This feeling was different from anything I'd ever experienced. It was part physical attraction, but there was also something that felt much bigger. Dancing so close to her–feeling her warm breath on my chest, smelling the shampoo in her hair–was so intoxicating that it confused me. Up to that point I had been dancing to all kinds of songs with different girls at the party, but nothing slapped me dizzy until that first dance with Dawn.

Stairway ramped up from its slow, acoustic

beginning to the famous Jimmy Page guitar crescendo, and we barely moved. Dancers around us separated and danced, but I didn't breathe for fear that the delicate spell enveloping us would break. We clung to each other, lost in a magical moment.

As the final notes of the *a cappella* ending ricocheted off the concrete floors, Mom flipped on all the lights. It was like throwing a bucket of water on two amorous dogs. The bright light shone in our faces, making us blink. The magic instantly evaporated. Dawn didn't even look at me. She simply turned and walked away. I noticed her cheek was slightly red from resting against my jacket lapel. I could still feel her warmth against me.

After all the pop cans and paper plates were swept up, I went home and lay down on my twin bed. It was several inches too short now, and my feet dangled off the edge. I pulled the pillow over my head and replayed the evening, song by song. The surprising thing was that some of the girls at the party seemed interested in me. I had no experience with flirting, but I was sure that's what had happened.

And yet, I could only think of Dawn and the sweet feeling of dancing slowly with her. I drifted off to sleep, still able to feel her cheek against my chest, her arms around my neck, and hearing *Stairway to Heaven* in my head.

Great Expectations

By the start of my junior year I had traded in my thick black glasses for contact lenses, and I wasn't nearly as awkward as before. I saved the money I earned over the summer and bought new clothes. I was even growing my hair longer, although I expected my step-dad to put his foot down any day and make me get it cut. I was a work in progress, but I was moving toward the acceptable end of the social spectrum.

At the end of October, something happened that impacted my life for years to come. The Friday before Halloween I was in my bedroom, reading a comic book and watching my 19" black-and-white TV. My bedroom television only got one channel, but that made watching TV easy. I either watched what was on that channel or did something else.

I was sitting in the rocking chair next to my space heater, reading a Mighty Avengers comic book and ignoring what was on TV. A lame show called *The Paul Lynde Halloween Special* was on.

I heard a thrashing guitar and looked up to see four guys in full black-and-white makeup, wailing on guitars and screaming like banshees. Behind them, flash pots were spitting fire fifteen feet high. The logo on the screen said KISS in huge letters. I had never heard of them, but I couldn't take my eyes off them. My older sisters got The Beatles on Ed Sullivan, and I got KISS on Paul Lynde.

As soon as the first song—*Detroit Rock City*—was done, Mom poked her head into my room.

"Jerry's on the phone for you," she said. "He says it's

important."

Jerry had been my best friend since I was eight years old. We shared a lot of interests: Marvel comic books, science fiction books, horror movies and shooting our BB guns. I trusted him more than anyone else and knew he always had my back.

I ran into the kitchen to tell him to turn on his TV, but when I picked up the phone, he was more excited than I'd ever heard him.

"Inmon! Do you see what's on TV? Holy shit!"

"I know!" I said. "Where did these guys come from?"

"I have no idea, but we've got to do something with this!"

"Like what are you thinking?" I asked him.

"I'm thinking we need to put on some makeup, get some guitars and be those guys!"

"Oh, that's an awesome idea! Aside from the fact we don't have any instruments and can't play or sing."

"Whatever, Inmon. I'm gonna go watch the rest of the show. Maybe they'll do another song. I'll see you tomorrow and we'll figure out how we're gonna do this. See ya!"

Jerry was the perfect complement for me. He jumped in with both feet whenever he saw an opportunity. He was the idea man, and I was the voice of reason.

The next day we got together and figured it out. We'd get our moms to make our costumes. We'd beg, borrow or steal some instruments, and we'd lip-sync to KISS records. That way we didn't need to know how to play or sing. Jerry's mom even said she had some wigs she could loan us, since our hair hadn't fully grown out yet.

Forming the group was Jerry's idea, so he got to pick who he wanted to be first. He chose Gene Simmons, *the Demon*. I was Jerry's best friend, so I got the next choice. I took Paul Stanley, *the Star Child*. All we needed was to recruit a Peter Criss and Ace Frehley. By the end of school on Monday, we talked our friend Kenny Schoenfeld into being Peter Criss, *the Cat*. Another friend, Bill Wood, would be Ace Frehley, *the Spaceman*.

Next, we needed a venue for our debut. When I saw the Mossyrock School District was holding a talent contest in January, I knew that was the ideal place to launch KISS II.

We decided to do *Detroit Rock City* at the Mossyrock Talent Show, since that was the song we saw them perform on TV. I was responsible for 'singing,' so I rehearsed for many hours. I didn't want to let the other guys down. Besides, it was fun being a rock star, even if it was only in my head.

By the time the talent show arrived, we were rehearsed and ready to go. I had the words down cold, and I'd even learned how to walk and jump in my platform boots, but we had a few problems. We hadn't figured out how to make flash pots like we saw on TV, and, even in makeup, I didn't look much like Paul Stanley. But we weren't going to allow a few details to slow down the juggernaut that was KISS II.

When the night of the Talent Show arrived, we hid backstage like nervous brides. We had our makeup and costumes on, and we wanted to make an entrance. After an endless parade of trumpet players, piano recitals, and singing trios, it was finally our turn.

We got into position behind the curtain and struck what we hoped was a dramatic pose. To someone who hadn't seen KISS on TV, I'm sure we looked like demented mannequins. The beginning of *Detroit Rock City* blasted from the sound system, but we continued to stand still, waiting for the driving guitar intro. When it came on, we rushed to our microphone stands and gyrated like we had lost our minds.

The kids in the crowd stood up and went crazy. The adults sat in lifeless shock. They looked at us like we were the final sign of the apocalypse. Performing on stage was a rush of epic proportions. I looked at Jerry to savor the moment with my best friend, but he was too busy playing a demon to notice.

When the song ended with one last chord crash, we froze in place, making what we hoped was an artistic connection to the way we started the song. We formed a frozen tableau while the teenagers screamed, stomped and whistled. The adults slowly shook their heads, trying to erase the preceding four minutes from their memories. We didn't know if anyone would think our act was cool, but even after the curtain was down, we could hear the kids in the crowd chanting "KISS! KISS! KISS!"

The crowd reaction made us sure we had won the Grand Prize, which carried the princely reward of $100. The high school principal, Mr. Alban, announced the winners. We grew more certain of victory with the announcement of each runner-up. He progressed slowly from 4th runner-up to 3rd, to 2nd, and finally to 1st, without announcing our name. I looked at Jerry and he smiled, certain we had won.

Finally the moment came. Mr. Alban paused dramatically and we heard a drum roll.

"The Grand Prize winner is... Becky Lenz for her piano recital!"

"Wait, what?" I asked Jerry.

I had no idea how this could happen. How could they give the Grand Prize to someone with talent when the acne-battling portion of the crowd obviously loved us?

We'd overlooked several factors, of course. This was a talent contest, and although our performance was creative and original, it wasn't really a talent. Playing *Moonlight Sonata* on piano required a lot more talent and dedication than jumping around like idiots in platform shoes and kabuki makeup. Also, the average age of the judges seemed to be 112, and it looked suspiciously like several of them had turned off their hearing aids when our music played.

Once we got past our disappointment, we remembered the roar of the crowd and the thrill of mimicking our heroes. Despite having almost no talent, we had taken the Mossyrock Talent Show by storm. In the end, it seemed being denied any of the prizes reinforced our credibility with the other kids.

Just like a real band, KISS II went through a major shake-up after the talent show. Ken Schoenfeld wanted out. He thought the talent show was a one-time-only performance when he joined. To him it felt foolish to pretend to play the drums in cat makeup. Our performance stirred up a huge response, and we weren't lacking for potential replacements. We soon settled on our friend Chip Lutz. Chip was a grade behind us, but was cool enough to hang with the big kids. Best of all, Chip could play the drums a little bit. Actual talent was a new and exciting concept.

We had plans for global domination, but they had to wait. I had entered a writing contest seeking "Washington's Most Promising Young Writers" and Harold and I were chosen to participate. Being selected meant we got to skip three days of school and go to Fort Worden State Park in Port Townsend for a writer's workshop.

I couldn't believe my luck, because life wasn't great at home. Mom's drinking was getting worse, and my step-dad's reaction to her drinking grew more pronounced. That led to very unpleasant evenings at my house. On most days, I tried to find somewhere to be until it was time to go to my room and go to sleep.

The chance to get away and hang out with creative, smart people for three days was a godsend. Fort Worden was an old military barracks where they filmed *An Officer and a Gentleman* a few years later. It overlooked the Strait of Juan de Fuca and had postcard views of the water.

When we arrived at the conference, we broke up into groups where we were assigned writing mentors. Ours was Alan Furst, and I'd never heard of him. His first book was about to be published, and he eventually became a best-selling author of espionage novels. It's hard to make the connection with the renowned author, but in 1977, he had long, dark, unkempt curly hair and dressed in workman chic: blue jeans and blue work shirts. He also had a very cool coat that he said was made out of a specific part of a walrus, but I have no idea if that was true or not.

He had just finished his first novel, called *Your Day in the Barrel*. He told us he got the title from an off-color joke and then he told us the joke, which made us feel grown up. He seemed skeptical about any of us making a career out of writing. During our first class, he said, "if any of you are here to become rich and famous as writers, you need to get over that idea right now." That seemed to hold true for everyone, except for him.

A girl from Moses Lake named Lorraine Lee was in our group. Lorraine was a couple months shy of graduating, and had already been accepted into the University of Washington. She was bright, sweet, and attractive. Harold and I argued over who was going to ask her out, though we both realized we had no shot. Before we left the fantasy world of the writers' retreat, I did work up the courage to ask for her address and phone number in Moses Lake. To my surprise, she gave them to me, along with a wallet-sized copy of her senior picture. It instantly became a prized possession. As Harold and I left Fort Worden for the drive back to Mossyrock, we were convinced we would never see her again.

Younger Girl

I spent the summer of 1977 in Auburn, Washington working for my oldest sister, Terri. Terri was eighteen years older than me and was smashing through the glass ceiling that hovered over women in business in the late '70s. She was a Vice President of Pay 'n Pak, a chain of home improvement stores.

Terri got me an entry-level job working as a clerk in the Building Department selling tools, roofing, and lumber. She also let me stay with her, her husband Jim, and my nephew Tommy in their beautiful house. When you sat on the diving board overlooking their pool, you could look straight out at Mt. Rainier. It was quite a contrast from my normal life on Damron Road in Mossyrock. I was happy to be away from the chaos that passed for normal life at home. Plus, I only worked three or four days a week. There was plenty of time to lie around the pool and goof off with Tommy, who was my nephew, but was only two years younger than me.

My goal that summer was to read through the great Russian authors. But about 200 pages into *Crime and Punishment*, I got sidetracked by the Commodores' *Brick House*. I spent much more time hanging out at discos than I did with my nose in a book. Tommy and I were optimistic that each trip to the disco would result in a life-altering romantic experience, but girls found us resistible.

By the end of the summer, I had a decent nest egg saved up, thanks to the free rent at my sister's house. It was enough to buy new clothes and a car. I bought a 1975 Chevrolet Vega before school started. The Vega wound up as one of the most maligned cars of the '70s. It was plagued by design flaws, including its aluminum cylinder block, which may explain why the dealer gave me such a bitchin' deal. But it didn't matter to me what the rest of the world thought. It was the most beautiful piece of machinery I ever saw. The best thing about it was that I was able to start my senior year driving to school instead of riding bus #9.

At the beginning of my senior year, the future stretched out in front of me with infinite possibilities. I wasn't exactly king of the school; I was a little too smart and uncoordinated for that. But, I had risen through the school's caste system to middle-class citizen, and that was enough for me.

Dawn had also changed a lot over the last two years. She had been profoundly shy when I met her. Now she was more outgoing and opinionated and I could see she was gaining confidence.

Two weeks after school started, I was surprised to see Dawn running across our yards and bounding up the front steps. She'd grown up a lot. She no longer looked like the young girl I had first met. Her strawberry blonde hair reached just past her shoulders and she was the perfect image of a foxy '70's girl with her bangs feathered on the side and an irresistible flash in her eyes.

She smiled at me with that unique combination of shyness and challenge – looking down bashfully while sticking her chin out at me defiantly–and said, "My mom wants to know, if you're not doing anything, can you come see her?" I pretended to think about it for five seconds and was rewarded with a classic teenage girl eye-roll.

"Yeah, sure," I said, and we walked next door.

I always felt like I was being granted an audience with the Queen whenever Colleen summoned me. She was confident and stern, and projected a regal air. She seemed to always be three thoughts ahead of anything I was thinking.

As soon as I walked into the house, Colleen said "Listen, Shawn. Dawn's struggling with her transition to high school. Her grades are starting to suffer."

I nodded and looked at Dawn with concern. Dawn was a smart girl, able to keep up with her studies. Plus, it was too early for Poor Work Slips to be sent home. It was possible that she had brought home a few subpar test scores, and Colleen wanted to nip the situation in the bud.

Finally, she asked me the question she had.

"So, would you be interested in tutoring Dawn?"

"Yeah, I could..."

Before I could agree, Colleen cut me off.

"Of course, we couldn't afford to pay you very much."

I knew that was true. Walt had been out of work for a while, and things were tight at their house.

"Sure."

"You'd be helping us out."

I didn't need much convincing. Whether I was getting paid or not, this was a win-win situation for me. I could score some points with an adult I wanted to impress and spend quality time alone with this beautiful freshman girl, who was now socially acceptable to date. I did the only sensible thing and volunteered to tutor Dawn for free.

A few days later, Dawn came over to my house for her first tutoring session. The dinner dishes had been cleared and Mom and my step-dad watched the news in the other room. I always saw her outside, so it felt more intimate to sit alone with her at my kitchen table. I became more and more aware of her presence–the way her knee occasionally rested against mine under the table and the warmth that radiated from her. If this were a movie, there would have been a romantic song and a first kiss. Unfortunately, it was my life, and I didn't possess that kind of confidence or moves. Instead, I sat there with her history book open, reviewing the chapter she was studying so I could quiz her. Dawn doodled on her peechee and listened.

There was a style of writing young girls used in the '70s that involved taking an individual letter, blowing it up like a balloon and making it look like furniture. When I looked up at her so we could go over the review questions, I saw Dawn had written in balloon letters, "LOVE–SOFT AS AN EASY CHAIR."

Seeing Dawn doodle the first line of a Barbra Streisand song made my heart beat faster. I'm not sure Dawn was purposefully flirting with me but I looked at her longingly, swallowed hard, and said "so, anyway, about these review questions…" The truth was that we had been friends for so long that I couldn't find a way to be romantic with her.

I had a grand plan for the Homecoming Dance my senior year. My plan was to convince Lorraine Lee to come down from the University of Washington to attend the dance with me. The idea of me, duded up in my floral print shirt and blue polyester leisure suit, walking into the Mossyrock High School Multipurpose Room arm-in-arm with Lorraine was too delirious to contemplate. I envisioned people all around us falling over from shock.

For no reason I can imagine–other than a weird desire to help the socially inept–Lorraine agreed to go to the dance with me. She said she would drive down after her last class that Friday. I offered to spend some of my hard-earned dollars on a hotel room, but Lorraine said she was willing to stay in our spare bedroom if it was okay with my folks. By some small miracle, it was. I think they believed this was all a big fantasy and Lorraine wouldn't actually show up.

They were right. She didn't show.

The day of the dance, Lorraine called me at home to tell me she had a family emergency, and she had to drive home to Moses Lake immediately. She wouldn't be able to come to the dance. I was denied my triumphant moment. I was crushed.

I had two choices. Swallow my pride, don my polyester finery and go to the dance wretchedly alone, or just say "to hell with it" and stay home and watch *The Love Boat*. I'm not sure why, but I decided to go. I might have been socially inept, but I was resilient.

On the way to the dance, I swung by Dawn's house to share my misery with her. When I got to the front door, I could see Walt and Colleen sitting in their chairs. Dawn was on the couch, looking comfy in jeans and a sweatshirt. Sure enough, *The Love Boat* was on TV. It all looked so homey and relaxed that it made me feel even worse, if that was possible. I nearly turned around and walked away, but I was made of sterner stuff than that. I knocked on their door, and explained my miserable circumstances.

I made a pretty easy target for ridicule, but Colleen and Dawn both took the high road and commiserated with me. After a few minutes, with me constantly flashing yearning glances at Dawn, I started to head to the dance.

Out of nowhere, Colleen had an idea. She said Dawn had been initially asked to the dance as well and they had bought a dress for her. But something came up, and she was also stranded without a date. It was acceptable for a senior boy to go stag to the dance, but not so for a freshman girl.

"Would you," Colleen wondered aloud, "be willing to take Dawn to the dance with you, as a favor to us?"

I didn't need much convincing–she was saving me from the misery of going stag.

"Ummm, sure."

This was such a saving grace, I was caught off guard. Colleen nodded at Dawn, and she shot up and off the couch.

Less than five minutes later she was back, shining and lovely in a floor-length antique white dress with a ruffle on the bottom. It had three-quarter sleeves and a small rose embroidered under the neckline. Colleen seemed to be glowing too, at the sight of her daughter in her lovely gown. She looked me square in the eye and said "Is this Dutch?"

At that moment, I was looking at Dawn and having a little difficulty breathing, let alone speaking or understanding the English language. Compared to the *Hookers R Us* formal wear that girls wear today, the dress Dawn was wearing was demure, but she took my breath away. At first, she looked uncertain, but when our eyes met and she saw the impact she had on me, I saw a small smile of satisfaction.

I thought to myself, *how the hell am I supposed to know if that dress is Dutch or not? I don't know anything about dresses!* I said "Yeah, sure, I guess so..."

Obviously disappointed when I didn't properly grasp her question, Colleen turned to Dawn and said, "Go get me my purse so I can get you some money."

Her meaning finally became clear and I was able to blurt out, "Oh, I thought you meant her dress! No, I already have our tickets to get in." I shut up to avoid doing further damage to myself. Colleen looked pleased that I had caught on. Dawn smiled at me, and Walt narrowed his eyes. He didn't seem to like the neighbor boy being dumbstruck by his daughter. I didn't blame him.

Dawn and I walked across her yard to the Vega. I held her door open and watched her tuck her dress inside the door. I closed the door and stood with light-headed awe. Twenty minutes earlier, I had been emotionally devastated. Now I was escorting the girl I'd had a crush on for months to the Homecoming dance.

The excitement leading up to it made the dance anticlimactic. Many of Dawn's friends were there, and mine were too, and that was two different groups of people. I realized right away there weren't going to be any

Stairway to Heaven moments that night. We danced, laughed and drank punch, but there was no real romance. Before the night was over, we posed for our Homecoming picture with the usual hokey autumn background, and had a really good time.

The drive home was less than a mile, which was way too short. I was enjoying a little alone time with Dawn as we cruised home. Kenny Nolan was on the radio, softly singing *I Like Dreamin'*. I pulled into my parking spot between our two houses and jumped out to open Dawn's door. I was hoping for a goodnight kiss, but I have a hard time keeping my mouth shut at appropriate times. Between the Vega and her front door, Dawn told me that Jeff, another boy from my class, had asked her if she wanted to go outside and smoke a joint. Both Dawn and I were so innocent I was actually surprised.

I made a connection in my brain and said, "Wait a minute. Isn't that a guy you went out with? You really know how to pick 'em." She narrowed her eyes and tossed her hair.

"He is, and I sure do," she said, shutting her front door softly but firmly in my face.

I'd like to say I eventually learned my lesson about when to keep my mouth shut, but a lifetime of evidence says otherwise. Considering my state of mind a few hours before, when I had trudged dejectedly over to Dawn's house, the whole night had turned out great.

I walked across the yard to my room and lay quietly down on my bed. I had just said goodnight to Dawn moments before and I was already figuring out when I could see her again.

Just a Song Before I Go

In mid-October 1977, I headed back to Auburn, where I had spent the summer living with Terri, my oldest sister. Auburn isn't much of a city, but it was many times the size of Mossyrock. It was only another half-hour to Seattle, so I grabbed any opportunity I could to go there. As an early graduation present, my sister Terri bought me a new suit and paid to have my senior picture taken by a photographer she worked with.

After making the 90-minute drive on Saturday morning, I met the photographer at a local park and we spent several hours dodging raindrops, trying to get the perfect shot. Any remnant of my summer tan was gone, and in the final pictures I looked pale and drawn.

Sunday morning, I woke up with the intention of watching the Seahawks play the Miami Dolphins with Tommy before I drove home. Just before kickoff, though, I felt like I might be coming down with something, so I left early. On the drive home, I felt worse, and by the time I rolled into Mossyrock, I was feeling awful.

I went straight to bed and slept from mid-afternoon until it was time to get up and go to school the next morning. I didn't feel any better when my alarm went off, so there was no way I could make it through a day of school. I ached all over, felt pain in my eyes, and my neck was so stiff I could barely move it.

Dr. Mom took my temperature and diagnosed a case of the flu brought on by standing in the rain getting my picture taken over the weekend. That seemed reasonable. I was sick all week, but by the time Friday arrived, I was feeling a lot better and knew I'd be ready to head back to school on Monday.

By Sunday I felt like my old self, and convinced Mom I was well enough to hang out with some friends at Craig Landes's house. Craig was a year behind me in school and was a good guy. It was a typical get-together, with a little music and lots of friends fooling around.

Eventually, we planned a snipe hunt. In a snipe hunt, the victim is stationed in a cold, wet environment outdoors, armed with a gunny sack to catch the snipe. Everyone else scatters and promises to drive the snipe toward the victim. Instead, everyone goes in and gets something warm to drink and waits to see how long it takes the victim to figure out what's going on. I was still feeling a little under the weather, so I passed on those festivities.

As the party was winding down, Jerry was messing around with his practice nunchuks. They were made out of hard foam plastic, but they packed a wallop on anyone taking a direct blow. Jerry and I decided to do a mock battle. As a finale to the play fight, Jerry swung the nunchuks hard at me a couple of inches off the ground, where I could easily jump over them.

I had either been slowed by my recent illness, or I was just slow, period. Whatever the reason, I missed the jump and the nunchuks slammed into my ankle. I felt a blast of pain and fell face first to the carpet. The pain was so incredible I thought I might turn to see my foot facing the wrong way. But when I looked, my ankle seemed normal.

Once I stood up to shake myself off, I realized my symptoms I'd had all week were back with a vengeance. It felt like the blow to my ankle aggravated my sickness, which made no sense.

I felt even worse than before as I made the short drive home. Mom demanded I go to bed as soon as she saw me walk through the front door. It was only 6:30, and I slept straight through until morning. I felt even worse by that morning, so Mom scheduled a doctor's appointment for that afternoon.

The 40-mile drive to the doctor's office was an endless fever dream in the backseat of her Chrysler. Once there, he gave me a thorough examination and asked to speak to Mom privately. They came back into the room with grave expressions, and the doctor told me I had viral encephalitis. When I told him I had no idea what encephalitis was, he told me it was commonly called "brain fever." I had never heard of that either.

Mom wanted to know what would help me recover. The doctor shrugged and said there wasn't really much in the way of treatment for encephalitis. I could be hospitalized, but that would mostly be for observation. I would either get better or I wouldn't.

"Well, I'm glad I spent $30 on an office visit to hear that," Mom said. She packed me in the car for the ride home.

I returned to bed when we got back to our trailer, and I didn't get up again for a long time. One of the symptoms of encephalitis is sleep. Each day I slept more than the day before. Eventually, I slept a mind-numbing 20-plus hours a day. There was no change in the other symptoms. Light of any kind sent a searing blast of pain into my brain, and turning my head was so painful I decided I didn't need to see anything that wasn't right in front of me. After six weeks, I was sleeping for several days at a time without waking at all.

After I'd been in bed for weeks, Mom brought Dawn over to my bedroom. Through the haze of sleep, I recognized Dawn's voice and swam up through layers of consciousness to try and talk to her. She had come to deliver my copy of our Homecoming picture and to see if I was still alive. I squinted and saw shadowy forms standing behind her.

"Who are all those other people with you?" I asked. Dawn looked over her shoulder and looked back at me with concern.

"I'm alone."

"Yeah, but..." I couldn't finish my sentence. Dawn's troubled brown eyes were the last thing I saw. I fell asleep and didn't want to wake up.

I experienced the oddest sensation of being awake but trapped inside my body. I spent hours walking around inside my own body, trying to find a way out. Eventually, I found a door at the top of a stone staircase leading deep inside myself. I decided to follow the staircase and see what I would find. It felt like it took days to descend those stairs. By then I had completely lost all sense of time.

Finally, I reached the bottom of the stairs and found a door identical to the one at the top. I didn't want to walk back up all those stairs, so I pushed open the door.

I walked into a room that was inviting and cozy, with stone walls covered by warm tapestries and a round window that overlooked a beautiful garden. Rays of sunshine poured in and sent shadows climbing up the stone wall. I saw a female version of myself sitting at a tall table next to a stone fireplace, writing in a book. But, she couldn't have been me, because I was me. This other, female version of me also looked like an elf. There's really no way to explain this experience without sounding at least a little bit crazy.

My elf-self looked up from her book and smiled. I sensed that she was expecting me and her smile soothed me.

"You can ask me anything you want," she said. I looked at her and thought for a moment.

"Why is there so much pain?" The act of speaking led to this question. I hadn't planned to ask it.

"Because your true self is perfect and cannot be harmed. You choose to put yourself into an imperfect vessel and live this life so you can experience pain. That's how you learn, change and grow."

"Uh-huh." I didn't have an answer for that. I turned and looked back toward the door when my elf-self spoke.

"I have another present for you before you go." She smiled warmly and opened her hands to me. "Perspective is everything," she said.

She turned back to the book she was writing in before looking at me one last time. She nodded toward the window. Beyond the window I could see green grass, flowers, and heavy branches of moss-covered trees reaching for the ground. I felt the peaceful embrace of the outdoors and the perfect light waiting for me there. I wanted to go there and rest, but she shook her head and said, "They're waiting for you."

I looked at the warm sunshine and felt myself irresistibly drawn to it. The light was so bright, I closed my eyes. When I opened them again, I was back in my darkened bedroom. I could still feel the warmth surrounding me. Mom was hovering over me, her face twisted in a sour knot.

I looked her in the eye and said, "Let I, who am a part of God, find the part of me that is a part of you." Understandably, that didn't calm her, and she scampered out of the room.

"I'm going to call the doctor!" she yelled.

She thought my fever was causing hallucinations, and maybe that was so. I have no way of knowing. What I felt in that room inside my head felt more real than anything I have ever experienced. I was never the same person after that fever-dream. I have seen things differently ever since.

Perspective is everything.

To this day, I don't know where the "Let I, who am a part of God..." line came from. It felt like I was quoting someone or something when I said it, but I've never been able to find that quote anywhere. Maybe it was one last parting gift from my elf-self still ringing in my ears when I woke up.

Mom was freaked out by the whole experience. She had always been a big reader of New Age books, and now she was convinced her real son was gone, and I had been replaced by what her books called a "walk-in"—a spirit that joins a life partway through. I was different after I woke up, but I was still just me at the same time.

In any case, when I woke up that day, I seemed to be over the worst of the encephalitis. I stayed in bed for another week to get my strength back, but I was getting better every day.

My dresser was covered with dozens of letters and get-well cards but my bedside table was almost empty. There was a glass of water, a little lamp and the Homecoming picture of Dawn and me. It came in a little cardboard frame, and I couldn't take my eyes off it. I looked pretty geeky in the picture, but Dawn looked so lovely it made my chest tight to look at her.

That last week in bed I spent more time pondering, "What does Dawn think about me?" than I did all other subjects combined. Before I could learn the answer, I had to regain my strength, which took until almost Christmas time.

Feels Like the First Time

I was sure I would bounce right back from the debilitating effects of encephalitis. However, the lingering symptoms combined with a month and a half of lying in bed meant a much slower recovery than I anticipated. Luckily, I had good relationships with my teachers. They would have been justified in giving me a whole trimester of Incompletes, which would have jeopardized my graduation that spring. Instead, several of my teachers took me aside, asked me a few questions about the relevant material and then told me I was "good to go."

Even with help from my teachers, the first few weeks of December 1977 were a whirlwind of cramming and makeup work, which left little time to pay attention to what really mattered to me those days, such as trying to get a date with Dawn.

As if I wasn't already busy enough, we had decided this was the time to resurrect KISS II. The band had undergone major changes over the summer. Six months earlier, Jerry, my nephew Tommy and I had all attended our first concert–KISS and Cheap Trick at the Seattle Center Coliseum.

Jerry and I had gone to the show in full KISS regalia, and we had an awesome time even before the first guitar note blew us away. KISS was on their *Love Gun* tour that summer, and Gene, Paul and Ace started the concert on illuminated risers that lifted up and hovered over the audience. The flash pots, light show and incredible energy KISS brought to a show overwhelmed us. I spent the first few minutes of the show in a hypnotic trance, repeating "unbelievable" over and over. I turned to Jerry and said, "It looks just like an album cover." Then KISS launched into an ear-piercing rendition of *I Stole Your Love* and that ended any attempt at conversation.

Then a funny thing happened. Jerry had played Gene Simmons since the day we started KISS II, but as the concert progressed, he moved toward the center of the stage where Paul Stanley was holding court. At the same time, I found myself watching Gene even though I had always been Paul. Gene had a serpentine, sinewy energy I hadn't been able to imagine before seeing his live performance.

Our minds were properly blown by the time the concert ended. We made our way back to the car and Jerry and I knew we had made a mistake when we first put KISS II together. Jerry should have been Paul and I should have been Gene. Jerry made a good Gene and a great Paul. At the same time, I made a horrendous Paul and a reasonably good Gene.

We started practicing our new roles as soon as school began. Then I got sick and everything ground to a halt for me. The rest of the band continued practicing in my absence, though, and Jerry got us our first gig. It was set for the Saturday after school let out for Christmas vacation.

The venue wasn't as exciting as the ones KISS played. It was the multi-purpose room in our high school and the crowd was roughly a hundred people, but we didn't care. Almost a year after we had first played at the Mossyrock Talent Show, KISS II was back. The rest of the world failed to take notice, but it meant a lot to us.

I don't know how we managed to talk the school administration into letting us perform that night. School was out for Christmas break and the teachers should have all been scattering to the four winds, but we talked them into opening up the school so we could massage their brains with KISS songs played at 100 decibels.

We arrived for our show at 3 PM, which was the earliest we could convince someone to open the doors to the school. We took down all the lunch tables and chairs to open up the room. This was rock 'n roll, and we didn't want anyone sitting down. No one told the custodian that the greatest lip-sync tribute band in Lewis County was going to perform that night, so the furnace wasn't on and the temperature inside was about 50 degrees. But we figured we'd heat it up through the sheer power of rock 'n roll.

We had genuine roadies by then, which meant we talked Jeff Hunter and Craig Landes into helping set up our sparse equipment. We had two huge, borrowed speakers and a reel-to-reel tape machine. Jeff even figured out a way to make flash pots, consisting of a scary mixture of a Folgers coffee can, bare electrical wire and gunpowder. I don't think they would have passed a fire safety inspection, but we were excited to have them.

From the outset, we received the same raucous crowd reaction as the year before at the talent show. This time it was even better, because it lasted an hour and a half instead of just one song. I didn't have the reputedly 7" tongue Gene did, but endless tongue exercises and sheer willpower helped me stick my tongue out a lot further. I was truly a suffering artist.

One other slight complication with this first show was that we hadn't thought to use smokeless gunpowder. After we blew off the fire pots during *Firehouse*, a billowy haze of smoke filled the room. Standing onstage, I couldn't see anyone past the front row. That was probably for the best, since the teachers didn't know we were going to do that and I didn't really want to see their expressions.

Dawn was there that night as well. I ran into her and a few of her friends before the show and I talked to them in my six-inch platform boots, costume with bat wings and a ratted-out wig with a top knot. Her friends seemed to eye me with a mixture of suspicion and awe. Being in KISS II was a whole new world for me. Although Dawn never seemed too impressed by the whole fake rock star thing, I knew it couldn't hurt if her friends were.

Before the concert, we sent out invitations to student council members from other schools, and a few of them showed up. By the end of the relatively successful debut of the new KISS II, we had interested parties in hot spots like Onalaska and Napavine. After so many false starts, it felt like we were finally on our way.

Before we could have further adventures in KISS II, there was Christmas to worry about. Each Christmas, my family went to stay with my sister Terri and her family in Auburn. This year I was able to drive up in my Vega by myself.

Staying with Terri, Jim, and Tommy in Auburn was something like an episode of *The Beverly Hillbillies*. My step-dad was a construction worker, and Mom was a waitress. My sister and her husband held high-profile jobs in the corporate world. They had a rambling, two-story home on a hill with a view of Mt. Rainier, and it was always decorated to the nines at Christmastime. Terri and Jim were always gracious and welcoming. Terri had outdone herself getting the house ready, and had arranged to have a choir come and sing Christmas carols to us.

After three days in the big city, my step-dad couldn't take it anymore. He and Mom packed up the Chrysler and headed back to Mossyrock. I stayed behind because I didn't want to drive the speed limit the whole way home, and I didn't want to risk a lecture from Mom.

Then a strange thing happened. I remembered it was Dawn's birthday, and I couldn't get her out of my mind. I sat in the basement and tried to play Strat-O-Matic College Football with Tommy. But between each play, my thoughts drifted to Dawn.

I had known Dawn for two and a half years by then. We spent hundreds of hours hanging out in our yards and shared one memorable slow dance on my 16th birthday. We'd gone on a last minute fill-in date at Homecoming two months prior. We were friends, but at least on the surface, nothing else. And yet, I couldn't get her out of my mind.

I had no idea why this inability to think of anything else took root at that exact moment. I only knew it was the truth. I also knew it was time for action. I needed to make something happen regardless of the consequences. I felt like I might explode if I just continued relying on fate to bail me out.

Before I left for home, I called Dawn. I dialed her number and was surprised at how nervous I was to call a girl I knew so well. After a few rings, Dawn answered.

"Hello?"

"Dawn? This is Shawn. Ummm... hey, I just remembered it's your birthday, and I was going to go out town and see *Star Wars* tonight anyway, so I was wondering if maybe you wanted to go with me."

I was so nervous I could feel my heart beating in my throat, but Dawn sounded as cool as ever.

"Yeah, okay. I'll ask Mom and Dad if I can go."

After a few seconds of muffled conversation on the other end, she said she could go.

I obsessed about Dawn and *Star Wars* on the drive home from Auburn. All I could think about was seeing her that night. It seemed that my Vega grew wings and flew me all the way home. I got back just in time to take a second shower and walk across the yard to pick Dawn up for our first real, planned, honest-to-God date.

After a complete interrogation by Walt and Colleen, we earned a stamp of approval and set out for the movie theater. Dawn was beside me like she had been so often, except now we were on a date. I was so nervous we hardly spoke on the entire drive to Centralia.

Since this was our first date, I wanted to make sure everything went smoothly. I didn't want to be late to the movie. I hadn't considered what would happen if we got to the theater before it was even open, though. As we pulled up to the darkened Fox Theater in Centralia, I realized the movie didn't start for more than an hour. I recovered by acting as if this was my plan all along. I turned to Dawn and smiled weakly.

"I got us to town early because I thought you might like to drive around and look at the Christmas lights."

She smiled and tucked her hair behind her ears. I loved it when she did that.

"Okay," she said. Her perfume filled my senses. It was *Babe* by Faberge, and the scent was becoming as familiar as her eyes. It was paralyzing me and I seemed to have lost whatever ability to think I had ever possessed. I sat in my own car with the girl next door I knew so well, and I felt like a stranger in a strange land.

We spent twenty minutes meandering past houses decorated with thousands of red, green and blue lights. It occurred to me that maybe the two showers, three times brushing my teeth and two times gargling mouthwash weren't enough. I pulled into 7-11 to pick up some Cinnamon Freshen-Up gum. It was my favorite gum, because it had a soft outer shell with a liquid center. The stores in Mossyrock rarely carried it, so I always picked some up when I was out town. My friends and I called it "cum gum" because it squirted when you bit down on it.

I held the door open for Dawn, and we stared at the dazzling array of gum and candy. I picked up a pack of Cinnamon Freshen-Up gum and Dawn smiled self-consciously.

"Do you know what my friends call that kind of gum?" We both giggled, and she stood on tip-toe and whispered the words in my ear. The ice was broken in an instant and it felt like we were just hanging out again, only this time in circumstances filled with wonder and possibility. I smiled at her and knew we had reached a new level of intimacy.

When we got back to the theater, we found a place to park right in front since it was still half an hour until the movie started. I was relieved to see the lights in the lobby welcoming us. Once inside, I told Dawn I wanted some Hot Tamales. I didn't, but I wanted her to feel comfortable getting something too. She said she didn't want anything, so I was stuck with an unopened box of Hot Tamales rattling around in my pocket all night.

We went upstairs and sat in the balcony, because that's where I'd always seen other teenagers sit when they were on a date. Once we picked out our seats and sat down, I was so distracted by the nearness of Dawn that the entire movie passed in a blur. *Star Wars* eventually became one of my favorite movies, but by the end of that night I didn't know the difference between R2D2 and Darth Vader.

I remembered nothing about the movie but everything about Dawn: the warmth of her arm brushing against mine and the feathery softness of her hair against my cheek as she leaned over to say something.

The ride home was happy and relaxed. We could finally talk and enjoy each other's company, just like we had so many times before.

The songs we heard on the drive home–*Tonight's the Night* by Rod Stewart, *Feels Like the First Time* by Foreigner, and *Dreams* by Fleetwood Mac–felt so appropriate. It was like the DJ at 62 KGW in Portland watched over us as our own musical guardian angel.

Our tires crunched over the gravel as I pulled into my parking spot between our two houses. *Let's Just Kiss and Say Good-bye* by the Manhattans was playing softly as I killed the engine.

I wondered what Dawn had thought about tonight.

Did she think of this as a date, or did she think I was just being nice to the kid next door on her birthday? I had too many pent-up thoughts and feelings inside me to let there be any doubt. As unsure of myself as I was, and as unsure of what, if anything, Dawn felt for me, I couldn't let the big hole of doubt exist inside me anymore.

Dawn got out of the Vega and walked toward her house. I threw open my door and met her at the front of the car. I reached out and touched her wrist gently, to stop her there. I had waited forever for this moment, but now I couldn't wait an extra fifteen seconds to walk her to her front door. She turned to me and we faced each other, standing in the exact spot where we had passed so many after-school hours together.

This time, though, the atmosphere was electric. I drew a long breath in the frosty air. I let go of her hand, reached up and touched her cheek softly. Her wide, brown eyes were warmed with flecks of gold. She stared at me, expectant and serious. I brushed the hair away from the side of her face and smiled at her, but I couldn't speak.

I moved my hands to her shoulders and pulled her the last little distance toward me and kissed her, softly and slowly. There were explosions in my head, and my heart raced. I felt for a fleeting moment like I was one with another person. It was one of the most perfect moments of my life and I instantly wanted more of that feeling.

We each withdrew a half-step with our eyes locked and fingers intertwined. Dawn cocked her head and gave me her drives-me-crazy half smile. Her bangs were a curtain over her forehead. I sensed satisfaction and a sweet happiness in her smile.

She turned away and walked across the frozen grass to her front door. I watched her until she disappeared around the corner of her house. Neither of us said a word. I stood anchored to the ground, unable to move. I watched her darkened house until the light came on in her bedroom window. Like a zombie, I turned and shuffled into my house, collapsing face first into bed.

I will almost certainly never know what Dawn was thinking or feeling as she went to bed that night. I know I laid there and let that feeling wash over me again and again, replaying the night, the thrill of being next to her in the darkened theater, our kiss, and that indescribable vibration I felt when I was close to her.

Dazed and Confused

Two weeks after I awoke from my bout with encephalitis, Mom slipped and fell on the ice outside our front door, fracturing her arm and wrist. That led to surgery, which led to complications and a lengthy hospital stay. The combination of pain from the injury and the anxiety she felt over being away from home while I was still recovering initiated a new downward cycle of depression and alcohol abuse.

It was obvious things weren't right with her after the New Year. As a long-time veteran of these wars, my plan was to hunker down and wait for the storm to pass me by. With only six months of my senior year left, I could see the finish line, and I just wanted to escape to the rest of my life.

On Friday, January 13th, I was in Mr. Warfield's Current World Problems class when a runner from the office delivered a letter addressed to me. Receiving mail from the outside world in the middle of class was highly unusual.

Mr. Warfield stopped his lecture and said, "Mr. Inmon, would you care to share with the rest of the class?"

"Um, no thanks."

"No, please. We'd like to know what sort of mail is important enough to interrupt our class."

The envelope was lime green, with a return address of Napavine High School. It was addressed to KISS II and Shaun Inmann. I was too excited to be concerned about the butchered spelling of my name. I tore open the envelope as Mr. Warfield and the rest of class watched.

"Dear KISS II members," I read aloud. "The freshman class from Napavine has made a unanimous decision to ask you to do a concert on February 18, 1978. To discuss all the details for your concert, please contact..."

"Okay, that'll be enough, Mr. Inmon, you can sit down now," Mr. Warfield interrupted. I wanted to keep reading. I couldn't believe a rival school would solicit KISS II. Their freshman class wanted us to come to their school and split the proceeds of a genuine/fake KISS II concert. It felt like we had made the big time.

The offer represented a great deal, since we would have gladly done it for free. Jerry and I were so excited that we were barely able to sit still during the rest of Current World Problems. Thankfully, it was our last class of the day. As soon as the bell rang, we ran out of the school whooping and hollering and acting like the young idiots we were. Jerry and I drove straight to his house to celebrate by making his mom suffer through several hours of *Christine Sixteen* and *Calling Dr. Love* played at increasingly high volume. She told us to turn it down only when the plaster started to shake loose from the ceiling.

After finally wearing ourselves out by pretending to be rock stars, I got in the Vega and drove home to tell Mom my big news. As soon as I opened the sliding glass door to the trailer my mood changed. Walking into the living room immediately doused my excitement. The trailer was completely dark, and the heat was turned off, which meant that I could see my breath inside. I knew Mom was home because her car was in the driveway. When I turned on the lights, I found a note from Mom saying she wasn't feeling well, but there was a casserole in the fridge for my step-dad and me.

Of course, I was a helpless teenage boy and had no idea what temperature or how long to heat the casserole, so I walked down the hallway and knocked on her bedroom door. I waited a moment and heard her weak, muffled voice. I creaked open the door and peeked inside. The curtains were pulled tight and the room felt dank and clammy.

"Mom, I'm not sure what temperature to cook the casserole."

"It doesn't matter. It just needs to be heated up. Go away."

A bad feeling crept over me. I stared at the floor, waiting for my eyes to adjust to the darkness of the room and listened to the near-total silence. I had one hand on the knob to leave when I heard what sounded like water dripping. But that was impossible; there was no plumbing in the bedroom.

"Mom? What's that noise? I hear water running."

"I told you to leave. Turn around, close the door and go."

Her voice sounded thin and lost. It didn't sound like her at all.

I fumbled for her hand in the darkness. It was deathly cold. I turned and flipped the light switch on. The light made me blink and when I turned back around I saw a horror show.

Mom was flat on her back, staring lifelessly at the ceiling. Her left arm extended off the bed. She had cut her arm in three different places, and an obscene amount of blood covered the floor. She must have been laying there for hours before I found her. Blood continued to drip from her arm and splatter into a pool on a blue blanket she had carefully placed on the floor to avoid a mess.

Her eyes were hollow and frightening, and her skin was a ghostly translucent. She looked like she had already died, but she was still moving. She fixed me with a stare and said, "I told you. Turn around. Close the door. Leave."

I stood motionless, trying to process everything, but my brain couldn't function. The floor seemed to tip away from me. I grew light-headed and leaned into the door. I felt a hand on my shoulder pulling me back upright. Only Mom and I were in the room, but I felt a firm hand keeping me upright.

I scrambled out of the room for the phone in the kitchen to call an ambulance, but ran face-first into my step-dad getting home from work. I couldn't talk, so I grabbed him by the elbow and pulled him to the bedroom.

He stood in the doorway, and shook his head in disgust. "If you were gonna do it, why did you have to do it this way?" he asked her.

I returned to find him picking up Mom's limp frame.

"Go get some towels and sit down in the back of the car."

I ran to the linen closet, then scrambled out to the Chrysler. He laid Mom across my lap and told me to hold the last of the towels against the cuts to try to stop the bleeding.

"It's too late," Mom said. "Just leave me alone and let me go." She repeated it over and over on the way to the hospital with the same thin, lost voice.

There was a hospital to the east in Morton ten miles away. Instead, my step-dad turned west, toward Chehalis, which was forty miles away. I don't know if he panicked and turned the wrong way, or if he wanted to give her the extra time to die. I thought I knew the answer, but I never had the courage to ask.

About halfway there, Mom closed her eyes and was quiet. She wasn't asking me to leave her alone anymore, but I didn't know if she had passed out or was dead. I didn't want to know, so when we pulled into the ER I just sat in the car and waited until two hospital workers lifted her off my lap. They put her on a gurney and wheeled her away.

Dad and I spent the rest of the night in the waiting room. I stared at her dried blood on my arms for quite a while before I thought to go into the bathroom and wash it off. Eventually, the ER doctor emerged and told us Mom was going to be okay.

"I'm supposed to report all suicide attempts to the authorities," he said gently.

"Do what you have to do," my step-dad said We walked out quietly and drove back to Mossyrock in silence.

It was after midnight when we pulled back into our driveway. The letter from the freshman class of Napavine High seemed like it had arrived a lifetime ago, instead of the ten hours it had actually been.

"When we get in, you just go to bed," he said. "I'll clean up the mess."

"Okay." I was incredibly grateful. I sure didn't want to clean up that mess. My step-dad slept in the guest bedroom after that night.

Mom entered a rehab center in Seattle after her wounds healed. She was forced to enter the rehab in exchange for not being charged with attempted suicide. That was fine with us. Neither of us knew what to say to her when we saw her, and she didn't say much either.

My Mom's hospitalization made the last few weeks of January really busy. I tried to keep the house clean and make dinner for my step-dad and me, which meant plenty of sloppy joes and Hamburger Helper. I was still carrying a full load at school and writing my entrance essay to complete my application for the University of Washington.

Looking back at those weeks, I am struck by how flexible I was. One day I was in the hospital waiting to find out if I was still going to have a mom, and the following weekend, I was back with KISS II arguing over what songs we were going to include in our set list for our upcoming show. Emotional amnesia is a handy thing to have.

I could have talked about everything that was going on in my life with Jerry, or Harold, or Dawn, but I didn't. I was embarrassed at what had happened with my Mom and I thought I was alone in the fact that my life that was so messed up, so I never said anything to anyone.

Before Mom came home from her 30-day visit in her 'quiet place,' KISS II gave its final concert in Napavine. The weekend of the show, my nephew Tommy came down to be part of the road crew. After I picked him up at the bus station in Chehalis, we drove home, unable to believe how much fun we were going to have.

And it was fun. That final show in Napavine was the culmination of everything good about KISS II. We had our choreography down, and each of us was very comfortable in our own persona. Attending that show had to feel like a mini-KISS concert. Since that's what we were going for, that was pretty cool.

Jeff Hunter held the whole thing together with spit and duct tape. That is, until about two-thirds of the way through the show. Right after Chip took center stage to sing *Beth*–always a highlight to the teen girls in the crowd–our sound system completely shut down. A real touring band might have had a backup plan. We were not a real touring band.

I don't know if anyone asked for their money back. I don't remember getting paid for the gig, so I guess it all came out all right for the Napavine High School Class of '81. KISS II started with a blaze of flash pots on the Paul Lynde Halloween special and ended in the Napavine gym with the buzz of a blown-out speaker.

It didn't generate a profit in dollars and cents, but KISS II made a huge difference in my life. I didn't attract the girls I dreamed about when I first put on the makeup, but I gained enough confidence to finally tell the one girl I cared about how I felt about her.

Magnet and Steel

Everything that happened during spring break my senior year was unplanned. I was going to stick around Mossyrock and see what trouble I could get into with Chip, Jerry or Harold. Then fate intervened in the form of a string of gorgeous pre-spring days. The week before the break we had blue skies, sunshine, and temperatures in the 60s–very unusual for March in Western Washington. The spectacularly nice weather caused people to do things they wouldn't ordinarily do that time of year, like leave their houses. That included Chip's dad, who looked at the first sunny day, checked the weather forecast, and decided it was time to replace the roof on their shop.

I happened to be hanging out at Chip's house when he reached this decision. He sized up my gangly frame.

"What do you know about roofing?"

"Absolutely nothing," I said.

"Are you afraid of heights?"

"Nope."

"Well, then, you're hired. I'll pay you five bucks an hour to help us."

Just like that, I was an apprentice roofer. Considering minimum wage was $2.65 an hour, and gasoline was about sixty cents a gallon, it seemed more than fair for an out-of-work high school senior with no skills or experience.

Of course, our top priority was to find music. We rigged a pulley system to pull the roofing felt and 3-tab shingles onto the roof. Chip had the bright idea to use the same system to haul his family's stereo up there. This was no small endeavor. The stereo and speakers were the size of a Shetland pony, and the sound reverberated around the whole neighborhood.

Chip and I made quite a sight, stripped to the waists, working on our tans. We threw bundles of shingles to each other while dancing to *Ain't No Half Steppin'* by Heatwave and *Slippery When Wet* by the Commodores. I'm sure we provided the neighbors with hours of entertainment.

Chip's dad shook his head when he saw us.

"You're going to break your damn fool necks up there," he said. But we worked hard and finished fast. That meant I was unemployed again, but that was okay, because I was unemployed with money in my pocket. After Mr. Lutz paid me the $80 I had earned, I put it together with all my other money and... still had $80. I was used to having nothing but lint in my pockets, so this windfall seemed like a fortune.

Suddenly, spring break stretched out in front of me, beckoning with endless possibilities. I made the snap decision to leave town. It wasn't that I wanted to be anywhere in particular. I just didn't want to be within the Mossyrock city limits any more.

The easiest thing would have been to hop in the Vega and trundle back up to see Terri and Tommy in Auburn. I could spend a few days going to movies and bumming around the Sea-Tac Mall. Instead, I wanted to enjoy a taste of newfound freedom and prove I could be out there on my own, without anyone's help.

As I was getting ready to leave for points unknown, I threw my backpack and sleeping bag into the back of the Vega. The Vega was a hatchback, which meant the backseat folded down to reveal what looked a lot like a bed. When I first drove it home and showed it to Colleen, she dubbed it the "Sin Bin." She intended this nickname as ironic commentary on my social ineptitude. Although it was intended as a joke, the name stuck. As I was preparing to leave on my epic voyage, Colleen came out to the car and presented me with two small embroidered pillows. One of them said "sin" and the other, of course read "bin."

I pulled out of my driveway with no idea where I was headed. I just drove and figured eventually I would realize where I was going. Somewhere in the back of my head, I had the idea I might drive down to Baker, Oregon to see my nieces, Amy Jo and Chrissy, who had moved away a few years ago. I was very close to them when they were little and I missed them. I didn't want to drive directly there, though. I wanted more out of the trip than that.

A series of random turns led me to admit I had subconsciously decided to go to Long Beach, which advertised itself as *The World's Longest Beach*. It wasn't surprising I would unconsciously drive there. My family had been vacationing there since before I was born and we usually made it to the beach at least once a year. Because I didn't get underway until Saturday afternoon, it was already getting dark by the time I pulled into Long Beach. I didn't have enough money to splurge on a motel room, and the temperature was dropping. My glorious plans of freedom seemed foolish.

I had always wanted to drive down to the beach, pull off on the sand where it was packed down enough that I wouldn't get stuck, and sleep with the sound of crashing waves in my ears. I turned off the main drag toward the ocean, found the high-tide line with my headlights, and settled in among the dunes for a good night's sleep.

I folded down the back seat and rolled out my sleeping bag, but I was too keyed up to sleep. I read a few chapters of *The Forever War* by Joe Haldeman with my flashlight. I finally got sleepy and turned off the flashlight and lay in my bag listening to the powerful ocean crash against the sand less than a hundred yards away. I felt content and peaceful, lying in the Vega's hatchback and enjoying my freedom. Slowly, I drifted off to sleep.

I awoke less than an hour later to a metallic tap-tap-tapping at the glass on the hatchback over my head. I opened my bleary eyes and saw two of Long Beach's finest, smirking and shining a flashlight at me.

"Excuse me, sir. There's no camping on the beach."

I considered explaining the difference between camping and sleeping. For once, I was smart enough to bite my tongue. I nodded and told them I would move on. I reluctantly crawled out of my warm sleeping bag and into the front seat.

As I re-started the Vega and steered away from the ocean toward town, I had no idea where to go next. My plan, meager as it might have been, evaporated with a few taps of an officer's flashlight on my window. I drove the deserted streets of Long Beach hoping for inspiration. Eventually, I saw an all-night diner. The pool of light from the window was warm and inviting, and I pulled in without thinking. I grabbed my spiral notebook, went inside, and sat down in a corner booth with a view of the deserted street. I was a pretty wild kid so I ordered a pot of tea. I intended to write my impression of the scrambled beginning of my trip. As soon as I opened my notebook, I discovered I didn't want to write about that at all.

All I could think about was Dawn.

There was a battle inside me as I sat there. I wasn't any more self-centered than the average teenager, but this trip was about me. I wanted to find out what it would be like to be on my own, with no one to direct me or look out for me. I wanted to discover what kind of person I was going to be when I was away from everyone I loved and cared about.

And yet, when all the other distractions in my life were removed, I couldn't think of anything but Dawn. When I let my mind wander, my thoughts gravitated straight to her. When I closed my eyes, she filled my horizon.

In one life-changing moment I made a decision. I couldn't take not knowing how Dawn felt about me anymore. I would rather know she didn't care about me at all than continue to live in the dark. It would have been nice if I'd had this epiphany when I wasn't 100 miles away, but I did the best I could with what I had. I opened my notebook and wrote a letter to Dawn.

> *Dear Dawn,*
>
> *I'm sure you're surprised to get a letter from me while I'm gone, but there are some things I want to tell you. We've been friends for a long time now, and I've always been more of a big brother to you than anything else. Lately I've been having feelings toward you that aren't "brotherly."*
>
> *As I was sitting here I realized something, and I want to say it to you right out loud. I love you. I suppose I started to love you quite a while ago, but it wasn't until right now that I realized it completely. I know it's strange telling you this in a letter, but I couldn't take another day going by without telling you how I feel.*
>
> *I don't have any idea if you feel anything other than friendship toward me. If you don't, that's OK. Just throw this letter away and I'll never mention it again. I'll be home in a few days and if you want to, we can talk about it then.*
>
> *Shawn*

I left a dollar on the table to cover my tea, folded the letter up, and stuck it in an envelope I found in my glove box. I drove to the deserted post office and mailed it before I could change my mind. I felt pangs of regret as soon as the letter slid down the mail chute.

Why could I not leave well enough alone and let

things be? So many bad things could happen as a result of mailing the letter. If I could have reached in and retrieved it, I would have.

By the time I mailed the letter, it was around 2 AM and I was exhausted. I drove to a rest area a few miles outside of town with a sign that said "please limit your stay to 8 hours." I figured I could handle that. This time I was asleep before my head hit the pillow, and I slept until the sun woke me up.

After a backwoods tour of rural Washington and Oregon over the next two days, I finally made my way to Baker. I was hoping to see my nieces. My brother Mickey had divorced their mom Sue years before, but I had always gotten along well with her and I knew she'd be glad to let me see the girls.

This turned out to be the first time my penchant for not calling ahead got me in trouble. When I pulled into Baker in the middle of the afternoon, I found a payphone and called the number I had for them, but there was no answer. After driving around and seeing what passed for the sights, I tried again. There was still no answer.

I remembered the girls' grandmother, Joy, had also moved to Baker to be close to them. I looked up her number in the phone book and dialed. When she answered, I asked her if she knew when Amy Jo and Chrissy would be back.

"Late Saturday night," Joy said. "They've gone to California for spring vacation."

Oops. I hadn't considered the possibility that I might not be the only one who traveled during spring break. Joy offered to let me come to her place and spend the night in her spare bedroom, but I declined. I hung up the phone, and considered the consequences of making a long trip without calling ahead. Then I remembered that this week was more about the journey than the destination, so I didn't consider the trip to be a waste. I had also written a heartfelt letter and sent it winging on its way home in advance of my return. Now my excuse for being on the road had evaporated and it was time to head for home.

I had mailed that letter early Sunday morning. It was now late Tuesday. I wondered if she had already received it. Did she know how I really felt about her? How long did it take for the mail to get from Long Beach back up to Mossyrock? These felt like the most important questions I had ever considered, but in those ancient days without instant communication, there was no way to know.

I didn't want to go home and face the unknown reception waiting for me, but I didn't have a choice. I drove straight to Mossyrock, making the drive in just over nine hours.

On the way home, I stayed awake by tuning into any AM radio station I could find. I heard plenty of classic songs on the trip home–*Baker Street* by Gerry Rafferty, *Sweet Talkin' Woman* by The Electric Light Orchestra, *Magnet and Steel* by Walter Egan. But more than any other, I heard that great flugelhorn anthem, *Feels So Good* by Chuck Mangione. To this day, I can't hear *Feels So Good* without remembering that drive, speeding through the dark with my windows down and my radio up.

I pulled quietly into my parking spot between our two houses well after midnight. All was quiet and dark at Dawn's house. That was exactly why I had planned to arrive home so late. I was giving myself at least one more day before facing my fear of complete rejection.

Always and Forever

It was after midnight when I walked in the house, but Mom was still awake, bustling around the living room. She was getting ready for a flower show, and it looked like Mother Nature had ransacked our living room. There were flowers, greenery, and ferns strewn everywhere. When Mom was coming out of one of her black periods, she did better when she had something to obsess over. Flower shows were better than the alternative.

Even though I had been away from home for the first time ever, she was so distracted she barely registered that I was back. She didn't seem inclined to interrogate me over where I'd been for the last five days. I would have had a hard time explaining my journey to her anyway. I answered a few innocuous questions and slipped away to the quiet darkness of my bedroom.

When I had approached home a few minutes earlier, I had killed the engine on the Vega about a quarter-mile up Damron Road and slid noiselessly into my parking spot. I kept a watchful eye on Dawn's window, but it stayed dark.

I woke up the next morning with a knot in my stomach, wondering if Dawn had gotten my letter yet. I ambled out to the Vega to clean it out from my epic journey. The car had picked up a little funk from serving as my kitchen, dining room, and bedroom. I had been in the car for less than a minute when I heard Dawn's screen door slam.

I acted as if I hadn't heard her come outside. I continued cleaning the Vega and humming along to the Al Stewart song on the radio. Dawn walked up and leaned casually against the door without saying a word.

I was good at reading nonverbal clues after a lifetime of living in an alcoholic household. I turned and focused on Dawn, looking for the slightest reaction. All I saw was her normal, placid face, staring back at me with unwavering brown eyes. I instantly knew she hadn't received the letter. If she had, I would have detected some sort of reaction. I had stressed about this moment for days, wondering what her reaction would be. Now that I was face to face with her, she gave me nothing.

I wasn't willing to go on playing the same waiting game. I had to find out how she felt. I didn't have the emotional wherewithal necessary to have a real conversation about feelings and emotions with Dawn, so I improvised.

"Hey, I'm going up to Auburn today to see Terri and Tommy. Do you want to come?"

Going to Auburn suddenly seemed like a very good plan. If Dawn and I were in Auburn, I wouldn't have to wait all day for the postal truck to come barreling down Damron Road with my letter. I didn't think I could stand to be inside my trailer watching Dawn, standing at the mailbox opening that letter.

Dawn was underwhelmed as always. She shrugged and said, "I guess. I'll go check with Mom."

She bounced in and out of the house in a matter of moments and yelled, "When are we leaving?"

"Right now. Let's go!"

I formed a plan while driving north on I-5. As we passed through Olympia, I nodded to a restaurant you could see alongside the freeway.

"That's The Falls Terrace. I've heard it's a really great place to eat." I acted like I was a connoisseur of restaurants despite having rarely eaten out in my life. I had only heard about The Falls Terrace after my sister told me about it.

Dawn pursed her lips and nodded. I pressed on.

"I think we should go out to dinner there sometime, don't you?"

This was such a strange, off-the-wall conversation for two teenagers from Mossyrock to be having that Dawn turned in her seat and looked at me through narrowed eyes.

"Okay," she said. "I guess so."

"Let's go there on April 29th!"

Since this was still March, that was a lot of advance notice for a date.

Dawn's eyes narrowed further as she eyed me suspiciously.

"Oh, so *sometime* is April 29th?" she asked. "Alright, we can go to dinner there on April 29th."

What she didn't realize was that April 29th was the date of our Prom. It would have been easier to say, "Dawn, will you go to Prom with me?" But at that age, I didn't know how to do things the easy way. My method of asking Dawn out was similar to the game Mouse Trap, in which the goal was to build a complex contraption that did twenty-five different things, with the end result being a cage that dropped on a mouse.

I looked at her, still slightly shaking her head at me and said, "Remember that date. April 29th." I turned the volume up on 950 KJR and waited for a special song. Just before Spring Break, the Prom Committee decided the theme for Mossyrock High School's 1978 Senior Prom would be *Always and Forever*. It was a huge hit by Heatwave.

My plan was to wait for it to play, reveal that it was the theme of the Prom, and that the prom was on April 29th. I switched the dial between every Top 40 station on the dial–first KJR, then KING, and then KLSY. None of them was playing *Always and Forever*. It normally played every ten minutes. But, of course, every station seemed to have launched a Heatwave boycott at that moment. I grew worried as I took the exit off I-5 to Auburn. I didn't have a backup plan if that song didn't play.

Eventually, we were at the turnoff to Terri and Tommy's house. I drove past it on purpose, continually changing stations and sweating a little. I drove around Auburn, relying on the fact Dawn had never been there before, so she wouldn't realize I was essentially driving us in circles. I was just about ready to forget the charade when KJR finally bailed me out. I reached down and turned it up as the notes I'd been waiting for filled the car. We were sitting at a red light, and I turned to her so I could watch her expression.

"Do you like this song?"

"Mmmm-hmmmm." She sat with eyes straight ahead.

"I do too," I said casually. "Oh, hey. This is the song that's going to be the theme of the Prom."

She frowned slightly. She was starting to make the connection.

"Yep, it is." I rambled on. "Did I tell you Prom's going to be on April 29th? Hey, since we're already going out to dinner that night..."

That moment is forever frozen in time for me. For once, she couldn't contain her emotions. She widened her eyes and her mouth drew into the smallest of smiles. She inhaled sharply and turned toward me. But I didn't need to hear what she was going to say. That expression of happiness and surprise told me everything.

"Are you asking me to Prom?"

"Yeah, what do you think?"

She stared at me expectantly.

"Well? Will you go with me?"

Finally, she smiled wide and wrapped her arms around my neck.

"Of course!"

Finally, I knew the answer to the questions that had

haunted me for so long. It didn't matter whether the letter arrived or not. I knew she was with me. I swelled with happiness. It isn't often you can pinpoint an exact moment when your life changes, but for me it was that moment. The best part was that I appreciated it, even as it was happening. It has lived in my heart forever.

The light changed, and I backtracked the last mile to Terri's house consumed with joy. Nothing else in the world mattered.

I pulled into Terri's driveway, opened the door for Dawn, and floated inside. I still hadn't mastered the art of calling ahead, so they had no idea I was coming.

Terri was home sick from work, but she insisted I bring Dawn upstairs to meet her. I had some trepidation, since Terri was a little unpredictable. I didn't want to be embarrassed in front of my new girlfriend, but I shouldn't have worried. Terri was funny and charming, and Dawn relaxed when Terri threatened to break out naked baby pictures of me and Tommy. Tommy quickly suggested we go to Seattle to a Laserium show to avoid potentially fatal embarrassment.

Laserium was held inside the planetarium at the Pacific Science Center, right next to the Space Needle.

There were a few seats in the back, but only old people sat in them for the laser show. Everybody else laid flat on their backs up front, staring straight up at the ceiling. Usually, there was a theme, like *Laser Floyd* or *Laser Doors*, in which they would play a collection of songs while the laser technician flashed laser beams all over the ceiling in time to the music.

Unfortunately, when we called for the Laserium schedule, we found out the first show wasn't scheduled until 5:00, which meant Dawn and I wouldn't get back to the Rock until after 9:00, which was pushing our luck. Dawn borrowed the phone to call home and see if we could stay out that late, but Colleen said "no," which seemed reasonable to me. I'd been a little surprised they'd let me take her on this little adventure at all.

As Dawn was getting ready to hang up, I could hear Colleen's voice on the other end saying, "That's a good thing to save for next time." As it turned out, that 'next time' would be many years away.

After watching a movie at the Sea-Tac Mall, we dropped Tommy off and drove blissfully home to Mossyrock. I let my foot get a little heavy on the gas and was cruising along about 75 miles an hour. My first hint of trouble was when one of the cars I whipped past pulled in behind me and accelerated to keep up. I looked down and noticed my speed for the first time. I let off the gas and eased back over into the right lane, but I was already busted. As I slowed down to something resembling the speed limit, the trailing car pulled up alongside me. It was an orange Datsun 240Z, and the driver was motioning wildly at me.

"Shawn, that guy seems to want you to pull over," Dawn said with wide-eyed innocence.

"Really? I hadn't noticed."

I had no intention of pulling over. I took a quick glance and saw a red-faced man with a walrus mustache signaling and holding up a badge. I played dumb and shrugged. There was plenty of open road ahead of me and an exit less than a mile ahead. I accelerated again, as if I might be trying to lose the plainclothes cop, but his Datsun easily kept pace with my four-cylinder Vega.

When we were nearly past the exit, I braked and swerved to the right. I was fortunate not to spin out. I slowed to a stop on the shoulder, and watched the glorious sight of the Datsun blur past as he continued down I-5. Dawn looked at me in shock and we both broke out in laughter. After a few minutes I pulled back onto I-5 and drove home, never going as much as a mile an hour over the speed limit. It was the most peaceful drive of my life.

After finally laying my cards on the table, everything seemed natural – even complete silence.

We arrived home ahead of schedule and went inside to talk to Walt and Colleen. If they noticed the changed chemistry between Dawn and me, they never let on. Dawn followed me outside as I left and rewarded me with a goodnight kiss. Our fingers interlocked softly and I stepped backward, giving her a final longing look. The more time I spent with her, the more I wanted to spend. I walked across the yard and stopped to stare up at the million stars arrayed across the Washington sky.

Lose Your Heart

I had friends I could rely on in the spring of '78. True-blue friends that would be there for me through thick and thin. My best buddy was Jerry, but I also hung out a lot with Harold and Chip. Aside from my three best friends, there were a lot of other people I hung out with at least occasionally, including Kenny Schoenfeld. Kenny had a '73 Chevy Nova with an incredible sound system. Although I couldn't remember him going out with any girls from Mossyrock, he went with girls in surrounding towns and did pretty well.

Soon after Dawn and I returned from Auburn, Kenny told me he was taking his latest girl to a place called Hollywood Hollywood in Longview. He asked me if Dawn and I would like to double date, which seemed like a great idea to me. A double date would take some of the pressure off of me to know what to do on a date, because I wasn't at all sure. I could tell you the number written on the underside of the starship *Enterprise*, but didn't have a clue as to what constituted normal date behavior.

Things started well that night. Hollywood Hollywood was a nice place, and definitely something you wouldn't find in Mossyrock. It was an under-21 disco, with a lighted dance floor straight out of *Saturday Night Fever,* and a sound system that shook the walls. It was fun hanging out with another couple and gossiping about everybody else at the club. Plus, it turned out that Dawn was a good dancer. There was something about being on a dance floor with her and watching her move effortlessly that made me feel good all over.

We left Hollywood Hollywood and headed back to the town where Kenny's girlfriend lived. When we reached her house, he jumped out quickly and winked. I knew what this meant. Depending on how lucky he got, he might be back in five minutes, or it might be an hour. There was no telling. I got the idea that Dawn and I had some time to kill in the back seat. I don't know if you've ever sat in the back seat of an early '73 Nova, but it makes for pretty tight quarters. It was even tighter for me, being a shade over six-feet-tall and all knees and elbows.

Someone with any coolness would have delighted in this situation, but I grew uncomfortable. Dawn sat beside me, calmly listening to the soft music on the radio. Somehow, I was intimidated by the situation. I lacked the confidence to take our relationship to the next level. Up to that point, we had shared two soft goodnight kisses, and those had gone fine. Now, sitting in a cramped backseat, I was paralyzed.

Those moments in that backseat were among the very few times when things didn't click for us. Everything felt forced and unnatural. That strange, vibratory sense of oneness I had felt with her on several earlier occasions was gone. For several minutes, I tried to kiss Dawn, and she did her best to help me along, but we both recognized the awkwardness of the situation. Eventually, we gave up and sat there. Several more songs played on the radio and Kenny finally returned, whistling a happy tune. It seemed that his night had turned out a lot better at the end than ours had.

The ride home was forty minutes, but seemed a lot longer. I was miserable by the time Kenny dropped us off. I figured my awkwardness had killed whatever shot I had with the girl I cared about. I knew almost nothing about the opposite sex. As we stood quietly between our houses saying good night, Dawn looked at me with understanding and acceptance. I was so wrapped up in my own misery I couldn't appreciate her concern. I mumbled a goodnight to her and walked across the yard to my trailer.

I withdrew from Dawn out of fear and concern. I avoided her for weeks, which was not easy since our bedrooms were within sight of each other. I was ashamed I wasn't enough of a man to take the situation in hand. Also, I was feeling that we were going down the path toward falling apart before we got started. In my warped teenaged mind, I was intent on staying away from her so I wouldn't further risk losing our Prom date. I had none of the emotional maturity needed to handle this situation. When it came to interpersonal relationships, my development may have stopped in grade school.

As April 29th and Prom drew closer, I gained some perspective on our bad date. Finally, just a week before the big day, things came into focus for me, and I realized what an idiot I had been. I remembered all the things that made me fall in love with Dawn—her strong and unique way of looking at things, her ability to make me laugh, and the fact every time I looked at her my stomach flipped over.

Just like we were starting over, I screwed up my courage and stopped Dawn as she was getting off the bus Friday afternoon. I asked her if she would go to Hollywood Hollywood with me again. I told her it would be good for us to go dancing again so we could 'practice for the Prom.' The weeks of separation had planted seeds of doubt that she was even going to Prom with me. I was relieved when she said she would go dancing with me.

I still feel butterflies when I think about that trip to Longview. It was a magical night. I can pinpoint the exact moment when I transitioned from "I think I love you" to "I have fallen in love with you."

I picked Dawn up early that Saturday night. We hadn't talked in several weeks, but everything seemed natural and comfortable. We laughed and talked the entire drive down. I realized the folly of having withdrawn from

Dawn, and regretted the loss of those precious weeks we could have spent together.

We wore light jackets in the cool spring evening. When we got inside Hollywood Hollywood, I took them over to the coat check room to hang them up. When I came out, I saw another kid standing and talking to Dawn. It looked to me like he was asking her to dance, which didn't make me very happy. He was just a 15-year-old kid, standing roughly 5'4". I wore the platform shoes I wore when performing as KISS II, which left me standing about 6'6". I walked up behind the kid, leaned over, and growled at him just like Gene Simmons. It would have served me right if he had hauled off and decked me. Instead, his eyes grew wide as saucers, and he turned and ran. Dawn cocked her head, raised her eyebrows, and said, "Was that really necessary, Shawn?"

We sat at a table next to the dance floor. We didn't talk much, because of the music playing at a hundred decibels. But we held hands and drew closer at every moment.

Then the DJ played *Always and Forever*. Dawn and I walked hand-in-hand to a darkened corner and danced. We had a little more swing than when we danced to *Stairway to Heaven* at my 16th birthday. I lost myself in the warmth of her body against mine. It was like an out-of-body experience looking into her unwavering, almond eyes. It felt like I was floating above my body a few feet, looking down at the two of us dancing.

In what seemed like a matter of seconds, *Always and Forever* ended. The music segued into *Easy* by the Commodores. I've never felt as grateful to a DJ for playing back-to-back slow songs as I was at that moment. Time was slippery though, and *Easy* was over before it felt like it had even started.

Our eyes locked intently. We had stumbled onto a moment of enduring importance. A sense of peacefulness washed over me. I wanted this feeling to last forever. As the final repetitions of *Easy* faded away, the DJ bumped the energy back up by spinning *Boogie Shoes* by KC and the Sunshine Band.

The other couples surrendered the floor to the wave of dancers coming on. But Dawn and I weren't ready to relinquish the sweetness of that moment.

As the new song thumped to life, we continued holding each other.

That was the moment. There was no more 'Dawn, I think I love you.' I knew. We didn't speak because anything we said would have detracted from what we were experiencing. We finally gave way to the jostling of the other dancers and left the club immediately after walking off the floor. The disco was too crowded, and we both felt a need to be alone together.

We drove straight back to Mossyrock. All the way home, I racked my brain trying to think of a place where we could go and be alone. Finding a place to park had never been a priority in my life, but now it was urgent. I didn't want to go up above the Mossyrock Dam, because that was where every other necking couple would be.

Dawn seemed unconcerned as we drove. When we got in the Vega, she leaned over and laid her head softly against my shoulder. She didn't move the entire trip home. By the time I turned off of Highway 12 toward Damron Road, I was getting a little desperate. In less than a mile we would be home, and that was the last place I wanted to be with an hour to go before curfew.

At the last possible moment, I saw a road off to the left that had a preposterous pair of signs reading "Doss Cemetery" and "Dead End." Did someone at the Highway Department have a sense of humor, or was it just a cosmic coincidence?

I turned up the gravel road toward the cemetery. As I made the turn, Dawn lifted her head off my shoulder, raised one eyebrow and snuggled back against me.

When we came over the rise at the top of the hill, everything was laid out before us. It was a clear night with a full moon. Instead of being eerie, it was perfect, bathed in shimmering silvery light.

Radio reception was generally poor in Mossyrock. but at the top of Doss Hill, it was crystal clear. I tuned in 62 KGW, set the volume low and put my arm around Dawn. We sat and absorbed the wonder of the moment. I was in exactly the place I was supposed to be. As we held each other, any lingering doubts about whether or not our attraction was mutual were erased.

We became so emotionally entwined that small concerns like our total innocence became what they should have always been—enhancements to our lives rather than detriments.

With just a few minutes before Dawn's curfew, the radio played the unmistakable opening chord of The Hollies' *The Air That I Breathe*. For the first time I really understood what the lyrics were about. There was nothing else in the world I needed.

Hot Summer Nights

The week before Prom was our coming out for Dawn and me at Mossyrock High School. I was a longtime observer of the mating rituals of high school life, and now I was part of them. Every time I saw her in the halls between classes, I would catch my breath, my heart would leap, and I would realize how lucky I was. It was a miracle I got any schoolwork done.

Every morning, I picked Dawn up before school and we rode around together until the bell was about to ring, forcing us to scramble out of the car and get inside. We hung out together at lunch and between classes, and I drove her home when school was out. I was very happy with this routine.

The week before Prom was busy. We couldn't go to The Falls Terrace in Olympia because I'd given away the money I'd saved. The denizens of Damron Road were not wealthy. In fact, most of us were struggling to get by, and that certainly applied to Walt and Colleen. Colleen never worked in the years I knew them, and even though he always seemed willing to work, employment was sporadic for Walt. Things were always tight at their house. So, when I asked Dawn to Prom, I was putting them in a financial bind. I imagined that the cost of a formal dress was probably beyond them.

Things were a little easier for me. I didn't have a regular job, but there always seemed to be odd jobs I could find—stacking lumber at Keen and Howard's lumberyard, helping a farmer clear the blackberries and brush from a field, or covering a dishwashing shift at the local diner.

Whenever I really needed money, an opportunity seemed to arise. However, there were limitations to what I could earn working at minimum wage jobs in 1978. $2.65 an hour didn't add up quickly.

I gave up on the idea of a fancy dinner at a nice restaurant in Olympia. Instead, I took the money I had over to Colleen to go toward the cost of a dress for Dawn when I knew she wasn't home.

It made me feel better about the whole thing, but by the time I was done buying the Prom tickets and a corsage, my pockets were empty. Dinner, even at McDonalds out town, would definitely be out of the question. I moped around the house, unsure of how to proceed. And that was when Mom came through for me, big time. She and my step-dad had separated again, and she was only working a few hours a week as a waitress. She didn't have any money to give me. However, she was a good cook, and offered to make dinner for Dawn and me on Prom Night at our house.

I would have much rather gone to dinner at a real restaurant than eat at our doublewide trailer, but I took her up on it. Mom offered to make the meal before or after the dance, whatever we wanted. I closed my eyes and pictured Dawn and I sitting in our little kitchen in broad daylight eating dinner. It didn't seem very romantic. So I opted for after the dance, which meant Mom would be up cooking dinner for two just before midnight.

Thanks to Carolyn Sprinkle and the Prom court, my attire for Prom Night was already arranged. When it came to the Prom court, Mossyrock High School did things a little differently. We didn't have a traditional Prom king and queen. We only had a queen. Whoever was escorting the Prom queen could maybe say they were Prom king, but nobody else gave them that title.

Several weeks earlier, Carolyn Sprinkle told me she had been chosen for the court. She asked me if I would be her escort. When she asked me, she said, "I know you're taking Dawn to Prom, but you can still be my escort, right?"

Just like that, I had gone from a high school oh-fer to having two Prom dates. Plus, both girls knew about each other and didn't care. The best part was that I didn't have to decide what to wear on Prom Night. I went to the Tux Shop in Chehalis and told them I was on the Mossyrock Prom Court. The next thing I knew, I had my tux. It was a cream-and-tan number with a gold-colored shirt with tan ruffles and an oversized white bow tie. It was just as hideous as it sounds, but in an era when Donny & Marie and Barry Manilow ruled the airwaves, we thought we looked good.

The day of Prom, I spent most of the day scrubbing myself and the Sin Bin. By the end of the day, it was a miracle either of us had any skin left. Meanwhile, I never saw a glimpse of Dawn, aside from one happy wave from across the yard. We were like a superstitious wedding couple before the big moment.

I was fanatical about my preparations for that day. I picked Dawn one immaculate red rose from Mom's garden to go with her corsage, and then soaked it in ice water for hours to make sure it would last as long as possible. In addition to washing and waxing the Vega, and vacuuming and cleaning the whole interior, I used Q-tips to clean all the pin-pricks machined into the vinyl seats. I wanted to make sure Dawn didn't get anything on her beautiful dress. In all, I spent about four hours getting the Vega ready for the big night. The ironic thing was we were going to be in it for less than ten minutes, since the school and the dance were less than a mile from our houses. It didn't matter, I wanted everything to be perfect.

After my second shower of the day, I struggled to get into my tux. I'd never seen one before and had no idea how to tie a bowtie. The cummerbund looked like a useless slingshot. With Mom's help, I eventually managed to get it done.

I can't say I looked handsome that night. I was still 6'1" and 145 lbs. with uncontrollably curly hair, but I looked as good as I was capable of on that day. When the time finally arrived to pick Dawn up, I walked the short distance across our yards. I stopped for a moment at the spot where we shared our first kiss after *Star Wars* just four months earlier. We had come a long way since then.

I knocked gently on Dawn's front door and Walt let me in. Walt and Colleen seemed relaxed and slightly amused to see me dressed in my tux. I stood ramrod straight and scanned their living room for Dawn. Colleen told me she would be out in a minute.

I sat gingerly on the couch trying to keep the wrinkles out of my pants. I was focused on making conversation when Dawn stepped quietly into the living room. Looking at her, I felt incredibly privileged to be her date. The girl I loved never looked more beautiful.

Dawn always took a less-is-more approach with her makeup. She didn't need a lot of help to look good. Although her hair was brushed until it glowed, there was no special up-do. She was my dream girl in every way.

We posed for a few pictures for Walt and Colleen, walked across the yard, and repeated the process with Mom at my house. As we were leaving for the dance, Mom took me aside and said "I don't think I've ever seen a more beautiful girl." I could only agree.

After arriving at Prom, there were still more preparations to make. I listened to the complex instructions of where the court was supposed to stand and when we were supposed to move. But I was distracted trying to catch Dawn's eye clear across the room. There were dozens of people standing between us, but it felt like we were alone.

Just before the ceremony started, Ms. Gehrman, the

teacher who was orchestrating everything, came over and told Carolyn she had been elected queen of the Prom. Since Carolyn was the queen, we got the honor of leading off the dancing on an empty dance floor, waltzing to Jim Croce's *Time in a Bottle*. In the 1978 Mossyrock High School Annual, there's a picture of Carolyn and me dancing, and you can almost see the word balloon above my head saying "one-two-three, one-two-three."

As soon as I was able to escape the literal glare of the spotlight, I made my way to the cool shadows and the table Dawn and I claimed. Prom flew by. We danced, hung out with friends, laughed and held hands under the table, and got our formal picture taken. At midnight, we drove home, glowing from the good time. I was sure the best part of the night had already passed, which just shows how wrong I can be sometimes.

As we pulled into the yard, I could see Mom lighting the candles on the table and scampering off to her bedroom. She stopped only to hit play on the record player, which dropped *Always and Forever* on repeat.

We walked into a room lit by a dozen candles, our song playing on the stereo, and dinner laid out for us on the table. I could tell Dawn was impressed by the amount of planning that had gone into dinner. I had thought I was letting her down by having dinner in our little dining room in the trailer. I couldn't have been more wrong. Nothing could have been better.

Dawn slipped her shoes off, I took her wrap, and we sat down at the table. Mom had learned a few things getting ready for those flower shows, because everything was perfect. We made nice noises about the great dinner Mom had made–Cornish game hens with rice stuffing, salad and dessert–but I don't think either of us ate more than a few bites. This was about ceremony, not calories.

It was pushing 1 AM by the time we finished dinner. I was sure the night was done. This was the girl who hadn't been able to stay out past 9 PM to see Laserium just a month before, and now it was the middle of the night. But, after adjourning to the living room, instead of getting her shoes on to go home, Dawn asked me if I wanted to dance. Every expectation for Prom had already been met, but I happily agreed.

I don't know how many times we danced barefoot to *Always and Forever*. Four? Ten? More? I have no idea. It was an eternity of loveliness.

After we had danced so long it seemed we had merged into one, Dawn stepped back.

I turned my head slightly to one side and raised my eyebrows, wondering if our night was ending. Then I stepped through the looking glass.

Dawn half-smiled at me, and a serious expression fell across her face. She reached gracefully up with both hands, pushed her dress off her shoulders and let it fall silently to the ground. This beautiful, innocent girl stood before me in the flickering candlelight wearing very little.

I was struck dumb.

Dawn sharing this unexpected vulnerability with me was more than I could process. Her shy smile widened, but whatever she was thinking, she didn't say. She held her hands out to me in a gesture of complete trust. She stepped forward into my arms once again. I suddenly felt overdressed, wearing my tuxedo jacket, ruffled shirt, bow tie and cummerbund. I held her face gently in both hands, scanning it for some clue as to why this incredible bounty had been given to me.

Candlelight reflected in her brown eyes and I took a moment to absorb her beauty. Small goose bumps made tiny blonde hairs on her arm stand up. I reached out and softly traced the curve of her neck down to the strap of her silky soft bra, slipping it off her shoulder. My eyes widened and I felt an involuntary sharp intake of breath.

Neither of us had spoken a word. For my part,

whatever power of speech I normally possessed escaped me when her dress hit the ground. I held her, trying to catch my breath. We took a few small stumbling steps and lay down on the couch. Laying there, her breath hot on my face, she was the fulfillment of every dream I'd ever had.

She put her arms around my neck and looked up at me, her eyes burning with intensity. For the first time, she said, "Shawn, I love you." The room faded away. There was no floor, no gravity and no reality.

"Dawn. I love you, too." I had never meant anything more. I was overwhelmed with love, looking deep into her eyes. She kissed me with the same burning intensity and then touched my cheek, looked down at herself, naked except for white panties with little teddy bears on them. Shaking her head gently, she said, "but, it's still 'no.'" I didn't need to ask her what "no" she meant. I knew. I told her immediately and truthfully it was still "no" for me, too. I loved her completely, but I knew we weren't close to being ready for sex.

We lay against Mom's floral couch, and Dawn helped me untie my bowtie and solved the mystery of my cummerbund. Soon, we were lying on the couch skin to skin, and time stretched out. I fell into her eyes and into her very spirit. It was the most fulfilling thing I had ever known.

We talked for a while and stopped. We laughed softly, caressed, kissed, shared pledges of love and devotion. Time became slippery. I was surprised to see the first rays of sunlight coming over the horizon.

I heard the door to Mom's bedroom open and the sound of her slippered feet coming down the hall. I'm sure she thought I was long since in bed. We froze and I said a quick prayer that we wouldn't be discovered and our night ruined. We were truly blessed that night, because the next sound we heard was the click of the bathroom door as Mom went in.

I scrambled around on my hands and knees looking for tuxedo parts. Before I had even managed to find my pants, I looked and saw Dawn smiling happily at me, as fully dressed as when I had picked her up for the dance. It was like a scene out of *Bewitched*. I didn't know it was physically possible to dress that fast.

We didn't want to push our luck anymore. She kissed me softly. With one last sweet smile and a wave, she was gone.

I stood at our living room window and felt so much love for her I cried. I watched her walk across the yard in the first light of dawn.

Love is Like Oxygen

I crawled into bed as the sun was rising, exhausted as I had ever been. I was also one happy boy. I'd had dreams come true the night before I hadn't even gotten around to dreaming yet. I had felt so much so fast that my spirit felt overloaded, as if I couldn't possibly accept anything else.

As late as it was when I went to bed, it took me a long time to get to sleep. I didn't want to let go of the vision of Dawn standing in front of me with her Prom dress at her feet. When Mom came into my room at 9:30 AM, I had been asleep at most a couple of hours. When I pried my eyes open, Mom was standing at the end of my bed with a very unhappy look on her face.

"Walt is at the front door, and he wants to see you." I understood the look she was giving me. It was a look that said *What have you done now, Shawn?*

I had been so caught up in the wonder of the moment the night before that I hadn't given a moment's thought as to what situation Dawn was walking into. Under Mom's steady glare, I crawled out of bed and pulled on a pair of gym shorts and a Mossyrock PE T-shirt. I tried to knock the cobwebs out of my brain as I glanced meekly at Mom. Whatever Walt had to say, I had a hunch I was going to need my wits about me.

When I got to the sliding glass door at the front of the trailer, Walt was standing on the front porch. Somehow, he appeared embarrassed instead of pissed off.

"Mornin', Walt," I said, waiting for the shit to hit the fan.

Walt handed me a piece of paper. I stared at it

dumbly, completely unable to comprehend what I was looking at.

"That's for you. I want you to have it."

I stared stupidly at the paper, waiting for the world to come into focus.

"I woke up early this morning at about 5 AM."

Oh, crap, this is going to be bad.

"I was sitting in my chair, watching the sun getting ready to come up and having my first cup of coffee when Dawn came in. She was so beautiful; walking in the door with the first light of the day peeking in behind her that it almost broke my heart. I sent her straight off to bed, but I was so moved at seeing her like that, I sat down and wrote a poem about it."

Are you freaking kidding me?

"Uhh. Thanks, Walt. Really. But, why are you giving it to me?"

"Well, when I asked her why she looked so beautiful at the end of such a long night, she just said 'Shawn.' So, I thought I should bring it over to you."

I had never been so relieved. I thanked Walt profusely, mostly for not killing me for keeping his young daughter out until sunrise. I said goodbye to Walt and turned around to see Mom, staring at me through narrowed eyes. I think she'd done the math, realizing if Dawn was heading home at 5 AM, we must still have been up when she went to the bathroom. Under her suspicious gaze, I went back to my room and collapsed across my bed. I slept the sleep of the dead and still-innocent until afternoon.

The rest of May 1978 passed in a happy, dizzying blur. Each of the moments we were able to spend together felt so rare and precious, I didn't want to miss a single one.

My friends felt abandoned by me, but there were times I hung out with them just like we always had. One weekend, Jerry's parents were out of town and we had the run of his house to ourselves. We didn't throw the biggest party Mossyrock had ever seen. Instead, we opted for a mammoth game of *Risk, the Game of World Domination.* We blasted our KISS, Pink Floyd and Kansas albums at an absurd volume and played *Risk* for thirty hours straight. If Red Bull or Jolt Cola had been invented in 1978, we might have lasted longer. Instead we crashed and burned midway through Sunday.

During this marathon of skill, tactics and aggression, I occasionally thought of Dawn. My life had been challenging up to that point. Dawn and I had created something that was positive. That weekend at Jerry's house, knowing she was just a few miles away, made me more confident about life than I had ever been before. I felt lucky to have her helping me emerge from the shell I had built around myself.

During this time, everything was easy and natural between us. The only challenge we faced was a predictable one: how to handle our racing hormones. On Prom night, when Dawn told me she wasn't ready for sex, I quickly agreed. I was a normal teenage boy with normal lustful thoughts. But I knew we weren't ready to go too far too soon. As time passed, we constantly revisited that plan.

Things progressed quickly. We advanced from being too awkward to properly make out in the back seat of Kenny's Nova to incredibly intimate moments. We knew where we were headed. When talking calmly and logically about going further, the answer was always crystal clear. We both knew we needed to wait a while, no matter how passionate and impatient we felt. If we were in this for the long haul, waiting a few weeks, months or years made complete sense.

For the rest of the school year, we were completely content to run off every chance we got to what we regarded as our spot—Doss Cemetery. There we held each with complete emotional intimacy, skin to skin and staring into each other's eyes. Looking back on that time from my more jaded perspective, it seems impossible that that's all we did, but it was.

The longer we were together, the more comfortable we were with each other. Gradually, the conversation changed. Each of us would say "Well, I know I love you, and you love me, so..." We were not the first teenage couple to think this way. At the same time, I knew what it would mean if we slept together and were discovered. It would almost certainly lead to separation, and no short-term pleasure was worth that risk.

Toward the end of May, *Saturday Night Fever* was playing at the Fox Theater. We heard so much about it from our friends we had to check it out for ourselves. We went to the early showing and were surprised when we walked out of the theater into a warm spring evening. It wasn't even dark yet. We looked at each other, tested the air, and knew we weren't ready to head back to the 'Rock just yet.

I had the brilliant idea to go to the drive-in over by the Southwest Washington Fairgrounds, where the Grade-Z horror movie, *The Incredible Melting Man*, was playing. It didn't matter what the movie was, because as soon as darkness fell and the movie started, Dawn slid into me. Within a few minutes, we were both panting with pent-up passion. Dawn looked at me with a deadly serious, heated look and said, "I think you need to take me out of here."

Forty minutes later, we were once again pulling into our familiar spot at Doss Cemetery. That entire drive, I remember thinking to myself, "Is this it? Are we going to do it tonight?" followed by, "Come on, Shawn, snap out of it, you know better than this!" As soon as we rolled to a stop, I opened the hatchback, spread out the blanket and we hopped in the back.

Dawn lay there with the leaf-filtered moonlight playing across her. She was the most beautiful girl I could imagine. Even so, the drive had allowed blood to flow back to the part of my anatomy that needed it most—my brain. We talked about music and the end of the school year, and waited for the fever to pass us by. When Dawn's curfew drew near, we drove down the gravel road toward home as innocent as we had been when we drove up it.

One of my happiest memories of that May happened one Sunday afternoon. Our backyard was pretty big, since our property was a little over half an acre. Beside the L-shaped garden was a spot where my step-dad had plumbed in a water spigot and a hose reel. This was my favorite place to wash the Vega.

I pulled the Vega up into the yard with the doors open and the radio on. Jackson Browne's *The Load Out* was playing loudly. I'd already soaped and rinsed, and was starting to dry it off when Dawn appeared. It was a warm spring day and she was wearing shorts and a halter top. The sun had been shining all day, but spring weather changes quickly in western Washington and the sky suddenly darkened.

The thought of rain just crossed my mind when I felt the first raindrop, the size of a nickel, splash warmly against my arm. I looked up to see a sudden squall upon us. Drying the car was suddenly less of a priority. Both our houses looked far away, so we dashed inside the greenhouse my step-dad built across the back of his workshop.

In the time it took us to run to the greenhouse, we were both soaked. Inside, the smell of potting soil, plant starts, and gardening chemicals was heavy in the air. The rain escalated quickly into a thunderstorm. It beat down with incredible force and noise on the tin roof of the greenhouse. The storm came on so fast it made us laugh with surprise as we stared out at the show Mother Nature was putting on for us. I looked at Dawn with her soaking wet hair and held her close. I sang the song *Rain on the*

Roof by the Lovin' Spoonful softly in her ear. I'd never felt closer to another human being, almost whispering the words to her. I was in heaven, and wished those days would never pass.

A week later I was at Dawn's house watching *Fantasy Island* with Dawn and her parents. I should say that Walt and Colleen were watching TV. Dawn was busy applying lip gloss and I was busy watching Dawn applying her lip gloss. This was endlessly fascinating to me, as it would be to most teenage boys.

It was a light, strawberry-flavored lip gloss that didn't have a lot of color, but gave her lips an alluring shine. I was thinking I would kiss the gloss right off her if Walt and Colleen left the room for even a moment. I don't know how long this process lasted, but Dawn was making quite a production of it. She would put a little on, then glance over at me, then put on a little more and glance over at me again, teasing me into oblivion.

Eventually, Colleen cleared her throat at us, which brought me out of my reverie. I don't know how long she had been watching us, but it had been long enough to catch on. She arched her eyebrow at Dawn and said, "Are you trying to hypnotize him?"

Dawn said "no" in the scornful way only a teenage girl can. But, of course, that was exactly what she had been doing. The innocence of innocents.

Slip Sliding Away

The most perfect month of my young life vanished as suddenly as it arrived. Just before graduation, I took a job working on a small farm outside of town, cleaning out stalls, feeding the horses and pygmy goats and spraying the fields for toxic weeds. It wasn't glamorous work, but part-time jobs weren't easy to come by in a town of 400. My job was as simple as life could get, consisting of moving horseshit and listening to mindless orders.

The only tricky part of the job was dealing with the pygmy goats, which had free range over most of the farm. The alpha billy's name was Adam, and he had a classic case of small goat syndrome. He may have been less than two feet high, but he walked tall and acted like the enforcer for the entire farm.

Apparently, he saw me as a challenge to his authority, because he had a favorite trick he loved to play on me. He would lounge around the barnyard, looking innocently one way or the other until I was lulled into a false sense of security. Just when I turned my back on him, he would lower his head and ram his horns into the back of the knees.

Anyone who has been hit in the back of the knees by a pygmy goat knows the applicable laws of physics. I was going down. Eventually I learned that walking around with my head in the clouds was dangerous, often resulting in me lying flat on my back in the dirt. I learned to listen for the *thump-thump-thump* of Adam's approaching hooves. Of course, it was harder to jump out of the way when I was carrying two buckets of pig slop.

Graduation was scheduled for June 2nd, but the powers that be at Mossyrock High unleashed us on the world a week and a half earlier. As a freshman, Dawn was still in school. Therefore, the outside world held little interest for me. If they had let me, I would have continued to prowl the halls until graduation forced me out.

Instead, I took the chance to work overtime at the farm spraying for Scotch broom, a noxious shrub that spreads quickly if not contained. That meant lugging a canister of weed killer on my back and spraying it on any suspicious-looking plants. Doing this job helped me decide to stay in school and find work that didn't require me to sweat unless the air conditioning in my office went out.

After several days of spraying, I had inhaled enough poison to kill my entire family. I was not feeling well. In fact, I was almost done spraying the last field when I found myself unexpectedly laying on my back, staring up at the wisps of clouds against the blue sky and wondering what the hell happened to my legs.

I was feverish and dizzy, but I thought I had simply ingested too much weed killer. I went home, showered and changed, and went to my baccalaureate. It was being held in the Multi-purpose Room. Outside, it was 90 degrees. It was even hotter inside, and before long I felt sick as a dog. Midway through the ceremony, the inevitable moment arrived and I passed out for the first and only time in my life. Fortunately, I stood between Jerry and Harold, who held me up.

I realized it was something other than the spray making me sick. After a quick visit to the doctor, I had an easy diagnosis: strep throat. The prescribed cure was to take some antibiotics, stay off my feet, and get plenty of rest.

Unfortunately, there was no rest on the agenda for the next several days. My graduation was the next night, then my *Star Wars*-themed Senior Party, which our parents had been planning for months. Two days after that, I would be flying to Alaska for the summer with Jerry.

When we made the plan to spend the summer bumming around Alaska, I had no social life and I didn't think I'd be missing out on much. Now, being away from Dawn for three months seemed like a horrible idea. I was dreading the trip with every fiber of my being.

My inability to have an adult conversation essentially cost me my longest friendship. As spring and my relationship with Dawn bloomed, I could have gone to Jerry and told him, "Look, man, I know our Alaska trip seemed like a good idea when we planned it, but now I just don't want to go, and I'll be miserable if I do go." I think our friendship had been strong enough to have withstood that.

Instead, I took the coward's way out. I buried my head in the sand and hoped fate would save me. With the trip just a few days away, no divine intervention had emerged, and it was too late to change anything, so I was preparing to go.

With all that on my plate, I knew I would never be able to get plenty of rest like the doctor had said. I took the antibiotics and muddled through the best I could.

Graduations are a bittersweet occasion anyway, but strep throat made mine impossible to enjoy. Standing in the fading sunshine outside our school gymnasium with the twenty-seven other graduates of Mossyrock High School class of '78 took the wind out of our sails. There seemed to be a common look in all our eyes: we were scared to death. Just a few days earlier, we had all been anxious as hell for this moment to arrive so we could find our destinies. Now, on the eve of that happening, it seemed that we would have preferred the hallowed halls of Mossyrock High. At least, that was how I felt.

That wasn't an option though, so we were nervously

preparing to go through with the ceremony. Several of the boys in the class had bragged they were going to graduate without wearing pants underneath their robes, but all of us were fully clothed. As we entered, we wished we were wearing anything other than heavy graduation robes. Inside the gym it felt as hot as surface of the sun.

During the thirteen years we had gone through the Mossyrock educational system, we hadn't been the most unified class. But on this night we were the model of solidarity. As we marched into the gym, at least a few of us were solemnly singing, "graduate, graduate, dance to the music" to the tune of Three Dog Night's *Celebrate*.

My primary focus was to make it through the ceremony without passing out again. I'm happy to say I accomplished that modest goal. I even managed to snag a couple of scholarships and made it to the podium and back without tripping over my robe.

As I walked to the podium to get my diploma, I looked out over the packed audience. I saw Mom and my step-dad, my sister Terri, and, toward the front, Dawn and my nephew Tommy, cheering loudly.

I could feel my perspective changing. I looked at Dawn and my throat tightened and tears welled in my eyes. Since I was leaving first for Alaska and then the University of Washington, it was hard to imagine what was next for us. I didn't want anything to change. I had been so happy being with Dawn these past months. But, change rarely asks permission before arriving.

At that moment, Tommy must have said something funny to Dawn, because the concerned look on her face changed into her sunny smile, and everything was right with the world again.

When the ceremony was over, Terri threw me the keys to her brand new Lincoln Continental.

"Bring her back in one piece, okay?" As cool as it was to have Dawn beside me in a shiny new Lincoln with a full tank of gas, and as much as I would have liked to party until the early morning hours, I was so sick I was home in bed by 10 PM.

I spent the next day packing for my flight to Alaska. Our flight left early in the morning. Since it took two hours to drive from Mossyrock to Sea-Tac Airport, we had to leave well before sunrise.

Of course, Dawn and I spent that last day together. That night, Dawn and I sat in our side yard again just as we had so many times before. This time, there was a knot in my stomach, and sadness behind our smiles. Finally, after staying out as late as we could, I walked her to her door. With one last lingering kiss, she was gone. Watching her front door close softly behind her, I felt so alone. Since our magical night at Hollywood Hollywood, we had only grown closer, but that was the moment our separation felt real.

Jerry's mom was going to be pulling into the driveway to pick me up in just a few hours. But I had no intention of trying to sleep. Instead, I sat at our kitchen table and got out one of my school notebooks. I wrote to Dawn with songs. It's always been the language that expressed my feelings best.

The first thing I did was write out a list of the songs we had listened to over the preceding months. Naturally, a simple listing of our important songs was not enough for me. Beside each song I wrote a note—where we were when we first heard the song, why I loved it, or why it would make me think of her forever.

Then, I tore out some sheets of notebook paper and stapled them along three sides, leaving just the top open. I wrote the lyrics from Heatwave's *Always and Forever* on the front and slipped the 45 we had danced to on Prom night inside.

I did the same thing with Peter, Paul and Mary's version of John Denver's *Leaving on a Jet Plane,* which felt completely appropriate to me.

I took the two records, the list of songs, and some bad poetry I had written since we'd been a couple, and put them together. I slipped quietly across the yard and passed under her bedroom window. I left everything on the top step of her front porch. I knew she would find it first thing the next day.

I was completely miserable. I had a strong premonition that I would lose her forever if I left. Jerry had been my best friend for ten years, and we'd been planning this trip and all the fun we were going to have for so long, there was no way I could let him down either.

Long before sunrise, I was waiting with my suitcase on my front porch when Jerry and his Mom drove quietly into my driveway. With no sleep at all and a heavy heart, I set off on what had once seemed like the adventure of a lifetime.

We flew into Anchorage, changed planes, and got on a puddle jumper that flew us to Kodiak. We thought my brother Mick was going to meet us and take us to the boat, where we were going to be working. But when we got off the plane at the tiny airport, we couldn't find him.

We made our way to the harbor and even managed to find the boat we were supposed to be staying on. There were only two small problems. The boat was in dry-dock, and there was still no Mick. By then it was getting late. I hadn't slept in two days and we were exhausted. We climbed aboard the boat, found a bunk and crashed.

We tracked Mick down the next day and he told us there had been some problems with the boat we had planned to work on for the summer, leaving it in dry-dock. Mick needed to make money, so he signed on with a different boat, one with no jobs and no room for us on that boat. The good news was that he said it was alright for us to crash on the dry-docked boat for a while.

Jerry and I had $95 between us, our leftover booty

from graduation. That was no small sum in 1978, but we knew our funds wouldn't hold out long. We needed to find employment in a hurry. We were going broke, living on a small boat with no power or running water. We could afford to feed ourselves for three or four more days, if we were careful.

The next day, we found work at a fish processing plant. It was every bit as exciting as it sounds. Jerry and I were the only non-Filipinos working at the fish processing plant. We quickly learned to cuss in Tagalog or whatever dialect they were speaking. The only English words the other workers spoke were "hey, fish" and it's polar opposite "ho, fish." Each phrase could mean a wide variety of things, depending on the circumstances.

The trip had gone nothing like we planned. Still, if I hadn't been so head-over-heels in love with Dawn, it could have been another grand adventure for Jerry and me. But, I was obsessed with Dawn, and I grew more miserable every day. Asleep or awake, she was all I could think about.

After a few days, I skipped a meal and used the money to call her. The long distance rates from Alaska to Washington were about a dollar a minute, so I knew we couldn't talk long. I was hoping the comfort of hearing her voice would ease my mind. Instead, the sound of her voice on the other end of the line made me feel worse. The mature, reasonable thing to do would have been to bite the bullet, repress my feelings, and continue to work at the fish processing plant until something better came along. I was neither mature nor reasonable.

On the eighth day of our trip, we were at the Kodiak library for a free screening of *Blazing Saddles*. It was the ideal movie to take our mind off our troubles. Halfway through, I leaned over and whispered to Jerry, "I'm leaving."

He looked at me with confusion, and I realized he

wasn't sure I meant that I was leaving the screening or leaving Alaska. But I didn't care. I got up and left my friend in the darkness. I was packed and ready to go by the time Jerry returned to the boat. I was planning on catching the last ferry back to Seward on the mainland, and then hoped to catch a ride back to Anchorage and a flight home.

I tried to talk Jerry into coming home with me, but he had no interest in bailing on our adventure. Although he was doing his best to understand, he was miffed that I was deserting him like this. He told me so and he was completely right. We talked for hours on the boat that night about our hopes and dreams. It would be the last meaningful conversation we would have for many years.

I quickly ferried to the mainland, caught up with Mick's wife in Seward, and talked her into giving me a ride into Anchorage. I turned my end-of-summer ticket into a right-now ticket, and I was winging my way back to Seattle several months ahead of schedule.

When I touched down, I called Terri at work and asked her if she would mind picking me up at the airport so I could go to her house and take a shower. It had been a week since I had seen either hot water or a bar of soap. I definitely felt sorry for the people sitting next to me on the flight home. Terri, being the best big sister ever, dropped everything she was doing, picked me up at the airport, and took me to her house so I could shower and wash my clothes. Then she went the extra 100 miles and gave me a ride all the way to Mossyrock.

It was early evening by the time we got home. I was so fired up to see Dawn I almost couldn't stand it. But, I couldn't just stroll across the yard and knock on Dawn's front door. I sent Tommy over to Dawn's first, to talk with her and to commiserate over my long absence that summer. After he was inside for a few minutes, I slipped behind the wheel of the Vega and gave my world-famous–

in my own mind–*Love Gun* rat-a-tat-tat on my horn. This was always my subtle way of letting Dawn know I was home.

Dawn threw her front door open and scrambled down the porch steps, wanting to see who had the nerve to play a practical joke on her. The angry look on her face gave me the impression that she tore outside to kick somebody's butt. However, when she saw me, she sprinted across the yard and flew into my arms. I held her fiercely for a long, quiet moment, and everything was right again.

Tommy, Dawn and I walked across the yard and stepped inside the house to see Colleen. But I was caught off guard by her cold glare. For some unknown reason, she was angry at me.

I couldn't have known what she saw from her perspective–the boy next door cancelling his summer plans simply to spend time with her young daughter. In the end, Colleen's opinion wasn't important to me. Nothing seemed important now that I was in Dawn's presence again, soaking her in.

Colleen overwhelmed me with questions. She wanted to know why I was home again so soon after leaving for the entire summer. She wanted to know what my plans were now that I was home. The answers seemed obvious, and I didn't have anything to add. I think Dawn was a little surprised by her mom's reaction as well, but she didn't pay her any attention.

"Dawn. Shawn. I want to let you know that things are going to be different now. We've been much too lenient with you, but that's going to change."

We listened in silence.

"There are rules to be obeyed, and if they aren't there will be consequences. Do you understand that? You will be seeing less of each other. You will have curfews, and if you miss them, you won't be allowed to see each other at all."

I nodded numbly. Dawn glared at her. The three of us

headed outside to hang out together. The overwhelming elation at seeing Dawn began to feel hollow. I had graduated, was preparing to leave for college and had plenty of freedom. Dawn was getting ready to enter her sophomore year. She was under the complete control of her parents.

Between ourselves, Dawn and I considered ourselves to be equals. To the rest of the world, we weren't. This discrepancy between how we saw ourselves and how others perceived us would lead to one difficulty after another.

Breakdown

Instead of spending June on a crab boat in the Aleutian Islands, I was landlocked yet completely adrift in Mossyrock. I had quit my job working on the farm, since I had planned on being gone for two months. It turned out that horse manure waits for no man, so there was no job waiting for me when I returned. I was broke and unemployed, but happy to be back with Dawn.

My step-brother, Russell, and my step-sister, Tylene, came to stay with us for a few weeks. We had the run of the place for most of the time they were visiting. Mom was working as a waitress again and my step-dad was at work all day. We listened to music, played yard darts, badminton, Hearts and Crazy Eights.

I hoped I could be friends with Colleen again. I missed the camaraderie of stopping by unannounced and talking with her. Mom believed that Colleen had orchestrated the beginning of my relationship with Dawn because she thought I would be a nice, safe boy that would look out for her during her freshman year. I could still be controlled pretty easily, especially in high school. My mom also thought that I was no longer useful to Colleen, so she would do whatever she could to get rid of me.

If that was what Colleen had in mind, she was probably right. I was very innocent and naïve. I'm sure I was easier to control than a normal teenaged boy would have been. When I left for Alaska, I'm sure Colleen hoped Dawn's mind–and maybe her heart–would be elsewhere when I returned.

Late one morning just before the 4th of July, Walt,

Colleen, Dawn, and I started the vicious dance we would repeat the rest of the year. Russell, Tylene, and I were out in our side yard throwing the Frisbee. We saw Dawn through her open bedroom window. The three of us wandered across the yard and stood outside, talking to Dawn. I'm sure we were talking louder than we needed to, cutting up and laughing. We were teenagers and that's what we did.

However, we didn't know that Colleen was asleep in her room, right next to Dawn's. Or at least she had been sleeping until we woke her up. She came into Dawn's room and yelled at us to leave. She immediately grounded Dawn from seeing me for three days.

She wasn't grounded from going places, or hanging out with her friends, or seeing Russell and Tylene. She was simply not allowed to see me for three days. I think Colleen and Walt knew this would bother us more than anything else, and they were right. I also think they had been planning to do this since the day I returned from Alaska. They were just waiting for a pretext to keep us from seeing each other.

Three days seems like nothing now, but at the time it seemed like an eternity to be without her. Russell, Tylene, and I hung out for most of the three days, but they occasionally hung out with Dawn while I went inside. It felt arbitrary and cruel to be shunned. On one of those days, Russell and I were hitting a badminton birdie back and forth in the side yard, just killing time and talking back and forth. Dawn was in her room with the window open, watching us play. I looked up to see her motionless silhouette. She turned her record player up loud, blasting *Love Hurts* by Nazareth across the yard. I didn't know if she was sending the song's message to her Mom, to me, or both of us.

Meanwhile, I had to find employment. The Vega was running on fumes, and I had no money to take Dawn anywhere. One evening, Walt walked around to the backyard where I was washing the Vega. He told me the DeGoede bulb farm, where he worked, was hiring.

"I could get you on if you want," he said. I looked around for Colleen, who was nowhere in sight.

"Really?"

"Yeah. I could give you a ride to work and back. That is, if you want to come with." He looked tired from a long day at work. I wiped the sweat off my forehead and shot a blast of water at the Vega.

I paused for a moment, but there was really nothing to think about.

"Yeah, that'd be great. Thanks."

"Okay, I'll tell them."

"Sure, I can start whenever."

"And look. Whatever's happening between us away from the job, it won't affect what we're doing when we're at work. Sound good?"

"Sure."

I was eternally grateful to Walt for getting me that job. Unfortunately, my career at DeGoede bulb farm was destined to be short. My job was to stand on top of a box at the end of a conveyor belt and sort good bulbs from bad ones as they rolled past me. This did not require a lot of brainpower. It merely required the ability to stand for long stretches without falling asleep. I constantly attempted to engage my fellow line-workers in conversation. I thought the day would pass a lot quicker if we played *20 Questions* or *Name That Tune,* or at least talked about something other than tulip bulbs. Mostly, I ended up talking to myself, which wasn't too rewarding.

Toward the end of a shift in the middle of July, I turned to walk away from the assembly line and wrenched my knee. I had been standing there without moving for so long I had forgotten I was standing on a box. That was enough to pull me off the assembly line. My promising bulb evaluation career was over before it ever took off.

I was not heartbroken. However, I was unemployed again, and slightly hobbled. Two lonely days after I hurt my knee, I was sitting in our backyard under my favorite cherry tree reading Robert Heinlein's *Stranger in a Strange Land* when Dawn came out her back door. She came and sat beside me, both of us leaning our backs against the trunk of the cherry tree and talked. It was like it was so often when we were together. Time grew slippery, and soon we were the only two people in the world. I felt something else too, something I wasn't accustomed to feeling at all. A feeling of trust spread over me, and I realized I could tell her anything in the world and she would keep safe both the secret and the secret-giver.

I found myself lying with my head in Dawn's lap, talking about my real father. He had died when I was five years old, and I never talked about him with anyone—not Mom, not my sisters or brother, and not my best friends.

Once I started talking to Dawn about him, I couldn't stop. Words poured out of me in an endless stream. When I finished, I realized Dawn hadn't said a word the whole time. She had just sat with my head in her lap, stroking my hair and listening. When she saw that I was done, she turned my head toward her, captured my wavering gaze and said "I'm sorry." I don't know why I chose that moment to talk about Dad, but I do know whatever peace I have about losing him springs from that day, sitting under the cherry tree with Dawn Adele.

My knee healed over the next few weeks, and I was able to find temporary work as a hay hand on a couple of farms. This job consisted of standing in a hayfield, picking up a hay bale, and pitching it onto a slowly moving truck as it rolled by you. This began as a simple task and grew much harder as the hay piled up on the truck's bed. Eventually, I was tossing 40-60 lb. bales up and over four or five other layers of hay. Then I had to run and get to the next bale ahead of the truck as soon as I tossed one, and be ready to toss it. There was no need to spend time at the gym when I was haying.

Haying put money in my pocket again, which meant Dawn and I could go out.

Eventually, we missed a curfew and we were not allowed to see each other again for a few days. It happened again a couple weeks later. It was an odd way to spend the summer, alternating between happiness and frustration, able to see Dawn but not talk to her.

It was like the sensation of walking on ocean sand as the tide went out. One moment it felt like we were standing on solid ground, but the retreating water sucked the sand right out from under our feet. It was a dizzying feeling and we felt like we could lose our balance and tumble into the sea at any moment. That meant whenever we could see each other, we clung to each other more tightly than ever.

Colleen eventually tired of giving us these paper-cut punishments and called us on the carpet.

"We've given you both too many chances already, and you've let us down over and over. That's over now."

I turned my head a little quizzically. I knew we'd been home a few minutes late a couple of times, but we were really innocent, as far as teenagers went. We didn't drink or smoke or do drugs, and even though we tended to jump out of our clothes when we were alone, we weren't having sex.

I glanced at Dawn to see what she was thinking, but she gave me an almost imperceptible shrug. Her eyes were serious and a little scared.

"If you don't follow the rules from now on, you won't see each other at all, ever." Colleen's eyes bored into mine until I had to look away.

"If you two aren't where you're supposed to be when

you're supposed to be, or if you break any of our other rules, we are going to ban you from seeing each other. Permanently."

Her anger was so severe that it didn't seem to be real. I had a tough time wrapping my head around this whole idea.

A few days later we made another trip south to Longview to go to Hollywood Hollywood. We stayed there longer than usual, because time got away from us a little bit. But when we left the disco, we still had plenty of time to get Dawn home before her curfew.

Once in the Vega, Dawn laid her head gently against me. She closed her eyes, as she often did, placing her trust in me to get us safely home. I took the familiar road back through Longview to I-5 and got back on the freeway to head for home. Unfortunately, I didn't manage to do the simplest part of the night, which was getting on the freeway heading north. Instead, I got on I-5 South, heading for Portland.

We had driven for twenty minutes when I looked up to see a sign that said "Portland - 15 miles." I couldn't believe what I saw. I gave Dawn a little shake and told her the bad news. Instead of being half an hour closer to home, we were that much further away. I took the next exit and booked it for home.

By the time we pulled into the driveway between our houses, Dawn was forty minutes past her curfew. I walked Dawn to her door, hoping to face the music right away. But it was dark inside her house, so I gave her a mournful goodnight kiss and trudged across the yard to my room.

The next day, I went to see Dawn and was met by grim faces. Dawn told me when she'd gone in the house the night before, everyone was asleep. But in the middle of the night, Walt and Colleen awakened her with angry yells. Dawn told me she thought the house had been on fire.

We got the usual rebukes. They were disappointed in us, and they felt they couldn't trust us. Only this time they looked pleased. They said that, since they couldn't trust us to follow the rules, we wouldn't be allowed to see each other at all.

I walked out of Dawn's house shell-shocked. I couldn't believe they would stop us from seeing each other forever. It didn't seem possible. In fact, I was sure they would change their minds any day. But as time passed, Walt and Colleen seemed completely happy with their decision.

Then, Russell and Tylene left to go back to Portland, my temporary jobs dried up, and Dawn was nowhere to be found. It appeared to be two long months until the fall quarter started at the University of Washington. I couldn't stand to spend the rest of the summer hanging out a hundred feet from Dawn, unable to talk to her.

Instead, I ran to Auburn to spend a few weeks with Terri and Tommy. When that didn't seem far enough, I drove south to California to see my sisters. I drove there slowly, using back roads and scenic routes. I drove Highway 101, which ran alongside the Pacific Ocean, all the way down Oregon. It wasn't the quickest route, but I craved motion, rather than actually arriving anywhere.

I kept my notebook open on the seat beside me throughout my trip, recording random thoughts and every song I heard on the drive. I was sure someday it would be very useful to know I heard The Electric Light Orchestra's *Sweet Talkin' Woman* six times during that trip.

My youngest sister Kristy was twelve years older than me, and she lived in San Jose. I drove there to see her, my brother-in-law Richard, and my two nieces, Kirsten and Andrea. San Jose was nice, but I was restless and needed to be in motion. So I drove to Los Angeles, to see my middle sister, Lana, and her husband, Curlee.

Unlike Randy Newman, I can't say I loved LA. It was

too big for a kid from the farmlands of Washington. While I was there, I went to Disneyland. Rather, I went *by* Disneyland. I didn't have enough money to go in and ride a roller coaster, but at least I could tell everyone back home I had seen The Magic Kingdom.

Although it was great getting to know my sisters as a quasi-adult, I felt a strong need to get home. The start of fall quarter at the UW was less than a month away. I needed to get to Seattle to find housing and register for classes. First, I had to find a way to see Dawn. I hadn't spoken with her in the weeks since I was banished by Walt and Colleen.

I managed to see Dawn a few times over the final weeks before school, but it never felt right. We had a lot of friends in Mossyrock, of course. They all knew what our situation was and they were willing to help however they could. Even when we did manage to arrange a meeting at a friend's house, Dawn was so nervous about getting caught that we couldn't enjoy being together. We never seemed to get past that initial "So, how are you?" stage. She was afraid every person that drove by was a spy for her parents and could never let her guard down. Having been so intimate in the past, it felt like being with a stranger by comparison.

I saw Dawn one final time before I had to leave for Seattle. It was the first week after Labor Day, and Mossyrock High invited all of that year's students, and graduates from the previous year, to come to the Multipurpose room to pick up their annuals and get them signed. In that crowded room, among all of our friends, it felt like every eye was on us. We were afraid to even stand close to each other for fear of getting caught.

Finally, I got Chip to slip my Annual to Dawn so she could sign it for me. I knew I couldn't sign hers because Colleen would check it, but I was desperate for any word from her. After an eternity, Chip finally brought the book back to me, slapped me on the back and left me to it. With my annual in hand, I couldn't take sitting there, so close but so far away from her. I rushed outside and sat down in the Vega, unable to wait any longer. I tore the book open and flipped straight to the back, searching for Dawn's looping cursive. She took up most of a page to herself:

> *Shawn,*
>
> *I really am sorry for all the things that have happened. I found out that I have some really good friends. I miss you so much. When I see you, I can only cry. That's what I have been doing all night. I love you so much - don't ever worry about that. You are my life and knowing that you love me keeps me from dying. All I can say is that I'm sorry... when I can see you, that same minute, I will be with you. Please - please - please - never forget me. I will never forget you. Always remember that I love you and always will. MY love for you will never end. YOU are the most important person in my life. I LOVE YOU!!"*
>
> *Dawn Adele*

I could see the emerging woman she was becoming and it was too much to take. I drove straight to our spot at Doss Cemetery. The evening light was beginning to fade. I sat reading what she had written over and over, wondering if I would ever see her again. *My Angel Baby* by Toby Beau was playing on the radio, but I reached down and turned it off. The music that I loved was too painful at that moment. The rain poured down my windshield as I sat alone in the same spot where we had shared so much happiness together. I mourned the loss of this time together for us.

The next day, I left for Seattle without seeing Dawn again.

Every Time I Think Of You

I tried out for the basketball team in fifth grade. That's when I learned being smart wasn't as important as being able to shoot free throws or throw a baseball really hard. Ever since that epiphany, I had looked forward to getting out of the small town God dropped me in and getting to a place where it was at least somewhat cool to be smart.

I had always figured that place would be the University of Washington. I dreamed about the UW for so long that by September of 1978 it had taken on the aura of legend. Now that the time to actually go there had arrived, that sense of anticipation was gone. The events of the summer and not being able to see or talk to Dawn sucked the joy out of leaving for school.

Terri's home on Aaby Drive was my halfway house on the journey to the UW. I showed up at her place with my scant belongings, including a suitcase my folks gave me as a graduation gift and my one piece of furniture–a tiny, wooden student desk–all crammed into the back of the Vega.

Using Terri's place as a base of operations, I went north thirty miles to the U-District in Seattle. My arrival was less than auspicious. I turned off I-5 at the 45th St. exit and headed east, not because I knew where I was going, but because that was the way the traffic was going. I passed the legendary Blue Moon Tavern on my left and Peaches Records and Tapes on my right. I rolled a few more blocks up 45th, keeping my eyes sharply peeled for the University. I didn't know how big it was, but I figured I should be able to spot it from my car.

When I stopped at a red light, Peter Brown's *Dance with Me* was blasting out of my AM radio. Seeing a cop standing on a corner, I turned down the music. I leaned toward the passenger side window and asked in my best non-hick accent, "Excuse me, officer. Can you tell me where the University of Washington is?"

He squinted at me, trying to decide if I was high, an idiot, or just pulling his leg. He shook his head and silently moved one step to his left. Immediately behind him, there was a giant sign that read "University of Washington." Only then did I notice the rolling campus, full of impressive-looking buildings, approximating what a major university might look like. I smiled grimly and nodded as if to say, "Oh yeah, I guess I could have seen that", and pulled through the light.

Although I had plenty of time to prepare for my arrival at UW, it was amazing how little I actually arranged in advance. I had no idea where I was going to be living. I didn't know what classes I wanted to take, and it was clear that I was completely alone.

I found a place to park and walked on campus for the first time. I walked inside Kane Hall–the first building I saw–and went to a bulletin board, pulling a tab from a room for rent ad.

I got lost fifteen times on my way to look at the place. When I found the address, it was clear there wasn't much to it. It was a 10' X 12' room in a basement with kitchen privileges. But at $100 per month, the price was right. And, it did have one advantage over every other place in the U-District–I knew where it was.

Luckily, the room came furnished. This meant it had a bed and a tiny, three-drawer dresser. After moving in my few belongings, I sat down on my new bed, suffering from culture shock. I was in a city of half a million people and I didn't know a single one. Worse yet, I couldn't get my mind off that one small-town girl 120 miles away. I was afraid I might never see her again.

If I had suffered separation anxiety a few months earlier in Alaska, I was in much worse shape now. When I was in Alaska, the separation was voluntary, and ended when I decided to return home. Now, home was a tiny cell of a room in a boarding house I shared with my five new best friends. I had no control over anything related to Dawn. Whether or not I ever saw her again depended solely on Walt and Colleen, and they seemed happy with the status quo.

I had been right about one thing. It was cool—and quite commonplace—to be smart at the UW. I also discovered that college women were a little more aggressive. Since I was having a hard time picking a major, I signed up for classes that would serve me well regardless of which direction I chose. My first class was Speech 101, and I met a girl named Karen.

I was so heartsick and in love with Dawn that I couldn't have been less interested in meeting someone to go out with. But Karen was nice, and we had lot in common. We were both small-town kids lost in the big city. During our first week of classes, Karen asked me if I knew a good place for under-21s to go dancing. I told her I did. There was a place called Reflections about twenty miles south of the UW in Renton. It was an underage dance club. When she suggested going there together, I didn't think anything about it. We were just two school friends hanging out.

By the fall of 1978, I was finally aware that disco wasn't cool. The Disco Sucks army was fully mobilized, and one of the FM rock stations, KISW, held a disco destruction moment every afternoon. I didn't care. I'd never been cool and I wasn't worried about it now. After school on the first Friday of the semester, I walked home and changed into the standard-issue disco clothes of the day—a silk shirt, tight pants, and a black silk scarf with a fringe. It wasn't a big improvement over the powder blue leisure suit I wore to Homecoming with Dawn the year before. I got a lot of grief from my new roommates at the boarding house. They were listening to the Sex Pistols and wearing T-shirts and ripped jeans, so my disco clothes made me an easy target.

Then Karen showed up at the front door wearing a little black dress, with long curly dark hair and a saucy smile. When she asked for me, the respect I got from my roommates elevated several notches. I knew she and I were just friends, but they didn't need to know that.

Once we got to Reflections, it was clear Karen and I were just friends hanging out. We danced together a few times, but we both danced more with other people. I spent more time watching everyone else dance and missing Dawn than I did anything else.

Sometime after midnight, Karen gave me a ride home in her powder blue VW bug. When we pulled up to the house on 23rd Ave, I told her to slow down and I'd jump out. Instead she asked if there wasn't a place we could pull in and park for a minute, because she wanted to talk to me.

I led her to a spot at the back of the house, and turned in my seat to see what it was she wanted to tell me. Before the tires even came to a complete stop, Karen was out of her bucket seat and into mine. Suddenly, the night took on a whole different flavor, as I found my lap full of a warm, pliant, beautiful woman. Without a word, she kissed me so hard I'm pretty sure my eyes crossed.

Even all these years later, I have no idea how or why this woman fell into my lap. I had started to outgrow the homeliness that plagued me throughout high school. But I wasn't exactly the movie star type, and Karen was very attractive.

I immediately grew uncomfortable. I loved Dawn. I didn't want to be with anyone else. I considered Karen to be a friend. I took hold of her shoulders and guided her back to her side of the car. I tried to talk but, as happens so often when I'm nervous, only babble and laughter came out. I don't know what I said, but Karen eventually got the message. She didn't seem bothered at all.

"Yeah, you're right," she said, smiling. "We should save that for a more special time."

It wasn't until I'd let myself into my little room and laid down on my bed that I realized what she meant. If I'd wanted to be less than a gentleman, I could have. In fact, I had to work pretty damn hard not to.

It was clear that college was a different world. It blew me away that this woman I barely knew would happily dive between the sheets with me. I still hadn't been with Dawn, whom I loved deeply and chastely. I knew my first time couldn't be with anyone but Dawn.

That night did bring me a gift of perspective, though. One day Dawn's folks were calling me on the carpet for not being in precisely the right place at precisely the right time, and a few weeks later, beautiful women were offering all kinds of potential delights. The problem was, I wasn't interested in any of them or any of those potential delights. I only wanted Dawn.

After that night, I avoided Karen at school for a few days. It was easy to do on a campus the size of UW. She seemed to get the message. She was still friendly, and not angry at me for my lack of follow-through.

I made sure never again to put myself in a position where I would have to deal with that kind of misunderstanding. I went to school, walked home, stayed in my room, and studied. I lived like a hermit for the rest of that quarter.

I had virtually no contact with Dawn those first few months in Seattle. I couldn't call her and we weren't even allowed to exchange letters. That didn't stop me from writing them and getting them to her, a complicated process. It required an entire underground railroad of our friends. Beyond those letters, which were filled with longing and strange ideas–*maybe we should just run away so we can be together*–I had no contact with her.

In early November, my friend Chip came up with a plan. He was dating Dawn's niece, Lori, who was living at Dawn's house. He had asked Lori if she wanted to go see the Commodores and the Brothers Johnson at Seattle Center Arena. As part of his clever plan, Chip told Walt and Colleen he had purchased a ticket for another friend who had been planning to go, but then backed out. So, Chip wondered, would they care if Dawn went to the concert as well?

Our plan was to have Chip, Lori and Dawn meet me in the U-District, and go to the concert from there. This charade would buy us a few sweet hours together. When Chip suggested it, I agreed before he could even finish explaining the idea. I couldn't get the thought of seeing Dawn out of my head. Aside from a few stolen moments here and there, I hadn't spent more than ten consecutive minutes with her since July. The idea of a whole evening with Dawn seemed like heaven.

The concert started at 7 PM, but I wanted them to get to Seattle as early as they could without arousing suspicion. I gave them directions to my place and we agreed to meet there at 4 PM on the day of the concert.

I was so nervous that I wasn't sure I would make it until 4 PM. I cleaned my room obsessively in anticipation. It had begun to look like a typical college student's room. By mid-afternoon, I had cleaned every surface I could think of, and sat nervously on the edge of my bed waiting for them.

When 4:30 rolled around and there was still no word from them, I thought I was going to go crazy. Our plan had hinged on one critical element–that Chip could find my place. As it turned out, he couldn't. Just when I was about to climb the walls, my landlord told me I had a phone call. I took the steps in two strides and was incredibly relieved to hear Chip's voice. They couldn't find my place, but they were at the Chevron station by Peaches Records and Tapes.

Ten minutes later, after breaking several traffic laws, I was there. Dawn and I finally had our reunion. Like always, as soon as we were together, everything else around us melted away. Before we headed to the concert, I guided them back to my place. All I had was the one room, but it was important that Dawn at least saw the place. I wanted her to be able to close her eyes and visualize where I was when we were separated again.

Back at my place, I stashed Chip and Lori in the communal living room for a minute while I took Dawn downstairs to my room. When we walked in to my room, *Always and Forever* was playing on the stereo. I was in favor of ditching the concert in favor of staying home and talking. But Chip, Lori, and Dawn were excited to go, so we loaded into Chip's dad's Monte Carlo, and headed for the show.

Once we got to the Seattle Center Coliseum, Chip and Lori headed into the insanity of the floor in front of the stage. Dawn and I found two empty seats at center stage at the very back of the floor. We settled in happily to watch the Brothers Johnson as they performed *Stomp!* and *Strawberry Letter 23*. As soon as we sat down, Dawn wrapped her arm around mine, laid her head on my shoulder, and acted as if she never wanted to move again. That would have been fine with me. Before we knew it, though, the Commodores came and went, and the show was over.

A feeling of darkness fell over me. We had looked forward to this night with such anticipation, and it was already over. We had no idea when we would be able to see each other again. This uncertainty made this parting monumentally sad. We walked out of the Coliseum holding onto each other so tightly that our hands were growing numb. Suddenly, we were greeted by a Christmas miracle, six weeks early. Snow had fallen the entire time we were inside the arena. It wasn't a typical Seattle snow-tease, either. It was already piled five inches deep. Traffic wasn't going anywhere. We couldn't believe our luck. There was no way Walt and Colleen would want Chip driving through this storm all the way to Mossyrock.

We got our story straight. It was the truth anyway, minus my presence. We found a payphone and Dawn called home. Of course, with two kids out in the wilds of Seattle, Colleen was already watching the news. She knew the story of the Blizzard of '78, rapidly paralyzing the entire city. Chip suggested he drive Dawn and Lori a few miles south to where his brother lived. He sure they would be safe and sound there until morning, when the snowplows had done their job.

Listening in on the conversation, I could tell Colleen didn't like this turn of events. What parent would? But, God and the weatherman had outflanked her. This was one situation she couldn't control, and she had no choice but to give her blessing.

I felt like a death row inmate receiving a last-minute reprieve from the Governor. I had been steeling myself for a separation again, and now the entire night stretched out in front before us, rich with possibilities.

Chip carefully maneuvered the Monte Carlo through the snarl of traffic, and we carefully negotiated the streets to his brother's house. Chip's brother didn't exactly welcome us with open arms. He was married with kids of his own. He wasn't prepared for four wet, bedraggled teenagers unexpectedly showing up at his house after midnight. As we walked through the door, I envisioned Dawn and me finding a quiet corner where we could canoodle. Instead, Chip's brother seemed to have missed the devil-may-care gene Chip had in abundance. He took his babysitting duties seriously.

There was a couch in the living room, and all four of us huddled together under a blanket, trying to get warm. Chip's brother went into the dining room and got an uncomfortable-looking straight-backed chair and sat down opposite us while his wife went back to bed.

One of our favorite songs was The Beach Boys' *Wouldn't It Be Nice,* which described waking up together after having spent the night together. We had often talked about how wonderful that would be, but we'd never envisioned it like this–Chip, Lori, Dawn and I all crammed under a blanket under the watchful eye of Chip's brother. We were exhausted by the excitement of the day and quickly fell asleep.

On the way out of the house the next morning, Chip's brother slapped me heavily on the back and said, "Sorry to be such a wet blanket last night. I didn't want anyone getting pregnant in my house."

With that ringing in my ears, I found myself standing beside the Monte Carlo saying goodbye to Dawn again. This day was clear and warmer and the snow was already melting. There was no good excuse for Dawn to remain in Seattle. We shared one last sad kiss, and the Monte Carlo disappeared south.

I had no idea if or when I would ever see Dawn again. I did know seeing her had made it even tougher to be without her again. Spending those few hours together, feeling the connection we always felt, and then losing each other only made the pain of separation much worse.

I stood on the sidewalk outside Chip's brother's house, unsure where I was. I started walking, looking for a Metro bus sign that might lead me home to the U-District. I finally found a bus going the right direction. As I rode, I realized I couldn't go on like this. There had to be a solution, and I felt like I was close to it. As I watched the miles slip by, a new plan cemented in my brain.

I needed to do something, and now I knew what it was.

I would ask Dawn to marry me.

How Deep Is Your Love

Wanting to marry Dawn and being able to marry her were two different things. She was under sixteen, which meant we would need her parents' permission. I was an optimistic person, but I didn't see that happening. Even so, I was convinced the answer was somewhere behind the impressive brick walls of one of the many University of Washington libraries.

In the weeks leading up to the Christmas break, I blew off my classes and spent the time trying to answer the question, "how can Dawn and I get married?" I hadn't even asked her if she wanted to get married, but I would cross that bridge once I found out if it was possible.

If I had possessed more common sense, I might have realized that if it was this difficult to arrange, it might not have been a good idea. Whenever I saw a brick wall standing between me and something I really wanted, I lowered my shoulder and hit it harder. There were times that this stubbornness served me well, but I'm not sure this was one of them.

At least spending all those hours poring over microfiche and dusty stacks of books served a couple of purposes. It distracted me from the pain of being separated from Dawn, and it made me feel like I was accomplishing something.

When I was finally getting close to admitting the loophole I was searching for didn't exist, I stumbled across a book that showed the minimum age to get married in every state in the Union. As I ran my finger down the list, I saw that every state had a minimum age of at least sixteen to get married without consent. There was only one exception.

The great state of Mississippi allowed girls as young as fifteen to get married, as long as you could pay for the marriage license and pass a blood test that showed you weren't first cousins. Since I knew Dawn and I could scrounge up the twelve bucks for the license, and there were no common branches in our family tree, I believed I had the answer. At least I had found one answer in one book out of the hundreds I had looked through. I didn't even want to give credence to the idea this book might be wrong. The most important feature of the book was that it agreed with me.

With this new information, a clearer plan emerged. I would buy a wedding ring and ask Dawn to marry me. If she said "yes," I would buy two airline tickets to the garden spot of Biloxi, Mississippi. Once we were legally married, I figured no one would be able to separate us again. As immature as it sounds, that was all I thought about.

What did I think the two of us—an 18-year-old college freshman and a 15-year-old high school sophomore—would do once we returned from Mississippi? Where would we live? How would we live? Even with a diet of Top Ramen and mac and cheese, I don't know how we would have managed, and I didn't give it much thought.

Instead, my first thought was about buying a ring. I hopped on a Metro bus to the U-District and walked into the first jewelry store I saw. I had seen enough commercials to know the rule of thumb was to spend two months' salary. Since my income in any given month was roughly zero, I wasn't sure where that left me.

I started by looking for the cheapest wedding set I could find. I had somewhere between $80 and $90 to spend, and I was hoping they would throw in the little box. I knew I was in trouble when all the rings I saw were at least $1000.

Eventually, I found a sympathetic salesman and told him exactly what I was up against. I must not have been the first dirt poor would-be groom to walk through the door, because he gestured for me to follow him as soon as I began telling him my story. He led me to a dimly lit corner of the store where he showed me a small tray of inexpensive rings. Then I saw it. Like in a Hollywood movie, I could hear a choir of angels singing and a bright spotlight shining on the most beautiful ring I ever saw. The wedding and engagement rings were both yellow gold. The wedding ring had a diamond chip that was barely visible. The part of the engagement ring that showed at the top of the finger had a wave design. The wedding band had exactly the same wave to it, and it fit snugly together with the engagement ring. It looked like Dawn and me. It was a perfect fit.

I was afraid to ask how much it cost, certain it was going to be more than I had. When the kind-hearted salesman took it out of the case, I saw a little tag with a price on it: $110. I was torn. On one hand, I did have that much with me. But with tax, it would take everything I had. In fact, if my Metro bus transfer slip expired before I could get to the bus, I would end up walking home. But none of that mattered. I had to have that ring.

I asked the salesman if I could bring the ring back if things didn't work out.

"No, son. I'm sorry, you can't. We can guarantee the ring but not the romance."

I was sure he had delivered that line many times before.

I stepped out of the jewelry store, fingering the velvet blue box they threw in. I stood under the awning as rain poured over the side, splashing noisily onto the sidewalk. I waited for the light to change so I could cross the Ave, and heard music coming out of an overhead speaker. It was

The Talking Heads' version of *Take Me to the River*. The words to the song didn't mean much to me, but ever since that day, I have associated that throbbing bass line with the feeling I had when I first heard it. It was an unsteady mixture of anticipation and dread. Fortunately, my bus transfer was still good, so I didn't have to walk home in the rain.

The next day, I put phase two of my plan into action. First, I dug around my room to find enough money to buy another Metro bus ticket. It was only forty cents, but that was more than I had in my pockets or my bank account. Once I had enough change for a bus ticket, I rode the bus south to Kent, where Terri worked. It was clear I would need more financial support if we were going to find our way to Mississippi.

Once again, I could have followed a more logical order. I could have made sure I had Terri's support before I blew my life's savings on a wedding ring. Luckily for me, Terri was not a typical older sister. She spent the first half of our lunch trying to talk me out of my crazy scheme. Then she relented after I showed her the ring and convinced her I was going to get married with or without her help. She even offered to let us take over the bottom floor of the house on Aaby Drive until we got on our feet.

It was an overwhelming offer. I had nothing to risk in this crazy adventure. I was a footloose college student with no money and no apparent future. On the other hand, Terri had plenty to lose by helping us. If things went wrong, it could have caused her a huge heartache and been a serious inconvenience.

After lunch with Terri, I found a few twenty-dollar bills in my pocket, which was more than enough to take the next step. Most importantly, I had her pledge to buy two round-trip tickets to Mississippi if the moment arrived.

The next day, my alarm went off at 4 AM. I had a long

way to travel and a definite deadline. My plan was to be waiting at the road that led up to Doss Cemetery when Dawn went walking by on her way home from school. That was my only real chance to communicate with her.

My Vega had been broken down for several months, and I hadn't had the money to get it fixed. If it had been running, I could have made the drive from Seattle to Chehalis in ninety minutes. Instead, it took me three and a half hours via Greyhound, since we stopped at every small town bus depot along the way.

I spent the time constantly checking the ring and taking a mental inventory. Was I in the proper frame of mind to make this life-altering decision? Probably not. Had I formulated a proper plan as to how to proceed if Dawn should say "yes?" Again, not so much. Did any of this dissuade me from my plan? Not at all. When I pictured my life, I could only imagine it with Dawn as the largest piece of it. Eloping was the only way I could see to make that happen.

By the time I got off the Greyhound in Chehalis, it was already past noon and I was in danger of missing my 3:05 deadline in Mossyrock. Luckily, I sat next to a nice lady whose husband was picking her up in Chehalis. They drove me to I-5 so I could hitch a ride, which eliminated close to an hour's walk. I had never hitchhiked in my life, but it seemed straightforward enough. After an hour of watching an endless stream of cars pass by, I was starting to despair about making it to Mossyrock in time. Just then an old sedan slowed down and pulled on to the shoulder of the entrance ramp. I was excited and ran up to the passenger side window. The driver was a man in his 50's with a week's unshaved beard, sucking on the stub of an unlit cigar. He leaned across the car and manually rolled down the window.

"Where ya headin'?"

"I'm tryin' to get to Mossyrock."

"It's your lucky day, kid. I'm going to Morton. Get in."

As soon as I clambered into the little sedan, I began to question whether it was really my lucky day or not. I immediately noticed a strong, pungent odor. It was a cross between a meat packing plant and the perfume my Aunt Pat used to wear. I hoped the smell wouldn't dissolve into my pores. I glanced in the back seat to see a heap of glossy pornographic magazines. I weighed the odds of him killing me and dumping my body in a field somewhere versus catching Dawn in time to propose. I just smiled, laughed a little nervously, and faced forward. When we made it to the blinking light at Mossyrock, I couldn't get out of the car fast enough.

I went straight to the spot where I was going to intercept Dawn. Mossyrock was a small town, and if I walked around, someone would see me and tell my folks. If anyone I knew saw me, I would have faced many uncomfortable questions about why I was in town and didn't come home.

I didn't want to make things more difficult for Dawn than they already were, so I stayed put. I stood behind some trees and waited and watched for Dawn to come down the hill. I had no way to let her know I was coming, so my appearance should have been a complete surprise. I waited with my heart in my throat. I hadn't seen or talked to her since the night of the Commodores concert. I was consumed with nervous energy and anticipation, knowing I would be with her for only a few moments.

My heart sank as I saw her coming over the hill. She walked as though she had weights attached to her shoulders dragging her down. I had been concentrating on my own suffering, but it was easy to see she had been hurting too.

Other girls Dawn's age were having slumber parties and dreaming about who they wanted to ask to Tolo. I was about to ask Dawn run away with me and start a new life. I was beginning to see what the problem was. It was me. The image of Dawn walking down that hill was so disheartening that I've never forgotten it.

Dawn crossed the highway and ran straight to me when she saw me. She gave me a sweet smile shadowed by sadness. We both felt the pressure of time. We had five minutes to talk before Colleen would suspect something was up.

I wasted no time.

"Dawn, I love you. Being apart from you is killing me a little bit every day. I've thought about this for months, and I can only think of one way to stop anyone from separating us again."

She stared at me solemnly, nodding her head. The ground around was wet and muddy, so I didn't drop down on one knee. I silently reached into my pocket and took out the little blue box. I opened it to show her the ring inside.

"Dawn Adele," I said. "Will you marry me?"

If this proposal surprised her, she didn't show it. In fact, she had seemed more surprised when I had asked her to Prom. Now, she just seemed numb.

She nodded again and smiled at me with more sadness than I could stand. It brought tears to my eyes. She looked me straight in the eye.

"Yes, Shawn, I will marry you." She said it quietly, but firmly.

She took both rings out of the box and handed them to me. I slid them on her finger. She took just a moment to turn her hand one way, then the other, seeing the way they fit together. Those rings looked better than I could have imagined.

I kissed her briefly and softly. She looked down at the rings on her finger.

"I love them, but there's no way I can take these home," she said. "Mom will find them."

"I know." I took the rings back from her, put them back in the case and slid it into my coat pocket. It was the last time Dawn ever saw those rings.

I held her tightly against me, feeling her warmth against my chest. Our too-few minutes were gone and she stepped away from me. She looked at me with mournful eyes and turned and walked away. She didn't look back as she walked around the corner and turned down Damron Road.

I stood at the base of the cemetery road with a lump in my throat, feeling more emotions than I had ever experienced at one time. The girl I loved beyond all reason had just told me she would take my side against all others, that she would stand with me always, and love me forever. I had no idea why I felt so horrible. The day I asked Dawn to marry me should have been one of the greatest days of my life. Instead, I felt selfish and sad, like I was putting my own happiness ahead of hers. That was not how I wanted to start our new life together.

I walked back to the highway and stuck out my thumb. Even if I got lucky and caught quick rides all the way, it would be after midnight by the time I got back to my room in the U-District. I had walked, ridden buses, and hitchhiked for more than eighteen hours to spend five minutes with Dawn.

After hitching back to Chehalis, I boarded a Greyhound for home. On the bus, I pulled a notebook out of my backpack and wrote, trying to capture the confusion I felt. It was simple stream-of-consciousness writing. I titled it "Where Can I Find the Strength." Sideways down the margin, I wrote, "I am ruining the life of the one I love."

I knew Dawn's life was more difficult and complicated because I was in it. I was preventing her from living a normal high school life, with none of the pressures and resentments she suffered from her parents on my account.

Still, I couldn't help but wonder what her life would have been like without me. The words I wrote illustrated the dilemma I felt so strongly: "Which is stronger/my need for you/or my desire for your best?"

I was getting closer to the answer.

Feels So Good

I got off the bus in the U-District in the middle of the night after my long strange journey to propose to Dawn. I was physically shot after being up for almost twenty-four hours. But it was the emotional and spiritual fatigue that I felt the strongest. No matter how I tried, I couldn't dispel the image of Dawn walking dejectedly down that hill, the weight of the world on her shoulders. That image forced me to see the toll our situation was taking on her. She wasn't the buoyant, happy girl I fell in love with a year earlier. I couldn't shake the idea I was the cause of this.

For the first time, I began to think I should leave her. It tore my heart to think that way. The idea seemed like insanity, and I would banish it to a dark corner of my mind. But it would fester there, growing stronger and confronting me again. I still believed we were destined to be together, but was it at any cost? When I closed my eyes, I could see her standing with me on the road to Doss Cemetery, wearing the rings that were now in my pocket. That thought warmed me clear through. Almost immediately, I would think, "but if she puts that much faith in me, how can I not do what is right for her?"

Those first few weeks of December 1978, I lived in the eye of the storm. Everything around me was quiet and routine, but I knew any day all hell was going to break loose again. I had asked Dawn to marry me and she'd said yes. But we needed to wait until at least her birthday on December 27th to carry out my crazy plan.

I made a few steps toward our elopement. I made sure Terri was serious when she agreed to front me the money for the airline tickets. I even talked to a travel agent about buying two round-trip tickets to Biloxi, Mississippi. But beyond that, I was just marking time. I should have buckled down and hit the books to catch up on my studies, but I couldn't focus on school at all.

During those weeks, I spent way more time beating the Aerosmith pinball game and bowling at the Student Union Building on the UW campus than studying. My grades suffered, but my bowling average climbed over 200.

My second Christmas miracle arrived on December 17th. I was on the bed in my little room on 23rd listening to Kasey Kasem count down the American Top 40, when my landlord yelled downstairs that I had a phone call. He reminded me I wasn't supposed to use the phone except for emergencies, but since I got a call about once in a blue moon, I wasn't too worried.

When I got upstairs and picked up the receiver from the dining room table, my heart leapt at the sound of Dawn's voice.

"We can see each other again!" she said.

"What?

"Mom and Dad said it was okay for us to see each other. Can you believe it?"

I couldn't. It took a moment to absorb her words. I leaned against the wall as though I had taken a blow to the ribs. What had looked like an endless, dark holiday season now opened up before me. I thought of going home to Mossyrock and being so close to Dawn and being able to see her without sneaking around. It seemed like a tremendous gift, and I would make sure I wouldn't waste it.

Best of all, the life in Dawn's voice was back. She sounded like the carefree, happy girl I always knew. It had been five long months apart, and now I wouldn't have to debate the difficult decision of removing myself from her life.

We only talked for a couple of minutes because long

distance phone calls were expensive in the '70s. Dawn said there would be conditions attached to seeing each other, but I couldn't have cared less. Whatever the price was, I would pay it gladly. I didn't care what conditions Walt and Colleen set forth. I would happily meet them. I had to see her as soon as possible. It was a Sunday night, but both the UW and Mossyrock High were out for Christmas vacation. There was nothing to stop me from going home the next day.

I hung up the phone and realized I hadn't asked her why we could see each other again, but it didn't matter. At that moment, only two things were important; I could see her again, and we didn't need to run away together. I knew I wanted to marry and be with Dawn forever, but I also knew it would work so much better in a few more years, after I had graduated from college and Dawn had finished high school.

Unfortunately, the Vega was still broken down, and I didn't have any money to get it fixed. However, one of my many roommates had flown home to Chicago to spend the holidays with his family. He loaned me his car for a couple of weeks on two conditions–I had to pick him up at the airport on New Year's Day, and I had to promise not wreck the car. I was more than happy to do both and I found myself the proud driver of a boring but functional Reliant K car.

I drove to Mossyrock the next afternoon. It was almost too delicious to think I would be able to just walk across the yard and knock on her door. I rolled into the driveway a little after 3 PM. I put in a quick appearance with the folks and made a beeline for Dawn's.

Colleen and Walt didn't welcome me with open arms. But I wasn't met with the level barrel of a .357 either. Just a week prior that would have been a real possibility. Walt and Colleen said they had reconsidered their permanent ban, and they were going to give us one more chance. They never said why, and I didn't want to stir up the hornet's nest by asking.

Eventually, Dawn told me my step-dad had come across the yard. There was a time when he and Walt were friends, but that visit was a rare occurrence since the trouble had started. He told Walt and Colleen that although Dawn was their daughter and they were entitled to do whatever they wanted, he was afraid keeping us apart would provoke us to do something foolish. He had no idea how right he was. I had no way of knowing if he actually got wind of our plans or if he was just making an educated guess. Either way he was right. For whatever reason, Walt and Colleen had relented, and we could see each other again.

Mixed in with that wonderful news was the idea there were going to be a lot more rules imposed this time. Dawn and I were not to be alone together. Instead, we were to be supervised at all times. Also, they wanted us to see a lot less of each other, which meant no more hanging around each other all day. Finally, they wanted me to know if there was a single rule violation that would be it. I would never be allowed to see Dawn again. It was just enough rope to hang myself.

It was such a relief to be able to walk down the street with Dawn without the constant threat of losing her again. Dawn's niece, Lori, was still living with her, which helped us avoid being alone. She was our built-in chaperone much of the time. Plus, if the three of us went somewhere, Lori was cool enough to give us a couple of minutes to ourselves to talk and catch up.

A few days before Christmas, Colleen casually mentioned she thought Dawn and I might be seeing too much of each other. I may be slow, but I am not completely incapable of learning. I used my head and hung out with Chip and Harold. Chip was a senior now and Harold was also home from college for the holidays.

Dawn and I did everything we could to make sure we didn't get banned from each other again. If we were going somewhere and Colleen told us to be home at 3 pm, I made damn sure we rolled into the driveway at 2:45. There was no way I was going to screw up this golden opportunity. It felt too good to have all that weight off both our shoulders.

Late on the morning of Christmas Eve, Dawn, Lori and I headed to the only entertainment option available in Mossyrock, the bowling alley. At the time, they seemed to have everything there—pinball machines, air hockey, pool, and even bowling.

As we were getting ready to leave, Dawn and I were sitting alone in the Reliant waiting for Lori to come out of the house. It was the ideal time to give Dawn her Christmas gift. As with everything we did over the winter, my budget was limited. My entire gift-giving budget for that holiday season was about $20. On my way south from Seattle the week before, I had stopped at Sea-Tac Mall and prowled the length of the mall looking for the perfect $10 gift. I found it at a small kiosk—a necklace that would look great on Dawn, and it was only $12.

When I had been standing in line to buy the necklace, I never could have imagined the scene in which I would later present it. Dawn and I sat inside the chilly car, the windows completely frosted over. It gave the whole setting a slightly surreal feel, as though we were all alone in the world.

"I got something for you," I said, and pulled out the white box. The necklace hung on a silver chain. It had silver on both sides surrounding a deep black stone. I didn't know what the stone was but I loved it. It was beautiful and somehow mysterious to my teenage eyes.

I couldn't read Dawn's expression as she opened the box. I thought maybe I had misjudged the necklace and she didn't like it.

"Do you like it?" I was momentarily crestfallen.

When she looked at me, though, I could tell she was moved. She nodded and smiled, and leaned over to kiss me.

That night, Dawn, Lori and I walked into town for a church cantata. It was snowing when we came out of church, just as it was the night of the Commodores concert, only this time there was no accompanying sense of dread. Lori stayed a few yards ahead of us as we walked home, and it felt like we were all alone in the snowfall.

Overtaken by the wonder of the moment, I stopped Dawn right in the middle of Damron Road and looked deep into her perfect brown eyes. There was snow accumulating in her hair. Her cheeks were frozen and she looked serenely happy. I brushed a few stray snowflakes from her hair and gently kissed her, unintentionally mimicking the kiss on the night of our *Star Wars* date almost exactly one year before.

We made some tentative plans to spend New Year's Eve together, but Dawn got a request to babysit that night. Money was tight, so Dawn never turned down a babysitting job. That put an end to our plans for New Year's Eve, but it had been such an unexpectedly wonderful week together we really didn't mind.

Instead of trying to set something up at the last minute with my friends, I elected to stay home with the folks and watch Dick Clark drop the ball. I spent the day re-categorizing my old comic book collection. Early that evening I was sitting in the living room, watching a rerun of *Alice,* when the phone rang.

"Shawn, it's for you," Mom said. "It's Dawn."

I picked up the phone and made every effort to be suave and debonair. "Yelloooow?"

Dawn wasn't buying the act. "Are you still a virgin?"

"Last time I checked," I said, floored by the question.

"Not after tonight," she said, "and that's a promise."

My head was spinning. Every teenage boy wants to hear their girlfriend tell them they want them in that way. On the other hand, we had just been allowed to see each other again, and I didn't want to screw up this opportunity.

My curiosity and hormones immediately silenced the little angel sitting on my shoulder. I thought to myself 'How will anyone ever know?' Overriding everything was how I felt about Dawn. When I closed my eyes and thought about being with her that way, my knees got weak. If Dawn wanted to be with me, it was going to happen whether we were ready or not. Damn the consequences. All these thoughts ran through my head in about a second and a half.

"Okay," I said. "Where?"

She gave me the address and told me to be there at 10 PM. It wasn't quite 6 PM yet and four hours seemed like an eternity. I strolled as casually as I could back into the living room, but Mom's radar was working just fine.

"What was that all about?" she asked suspiciously.

I shrugged my shoulders sullenly.

"It was nothing, Mom." I told her I had changed my mind and decided to go hang out with friends. Just like that, I lied to my Mom. My head was so full of wonder and questions that a quick fib seemed like the least of my worries.

I retreated to my bedroom to avoid Mom's probing glances and picked up the book I was reading. But alien invasions no longer held my interest, and I lay on my bed in silence. I stared at the ceiling and tried to make sense of what Dawn and I were about to do. After several hours of the deepest thought I was capable of, I was no closer to any answers.

Dawn and I had more or less settled the sex question a long time before, and had decided to wait. However, since we had been separated from each other, and with another separation hanging over our head like the Sword of Damocles, the question seemed less settled than before. I didn't know what was happening with Dawn or what she was thinking. Ultimately, it didn't matter. If she wanted me, I was going to be there.

After killing as much time as I could, I took a bath in the same little bathtub I'd been bathing in since I was a little boy. I lay in that tub full of hot water sprinkled with Jovan Musk cologne thinking "Is this really it?" It felt like my whole world was about to change.

I parked on the street in front of the little house just a few minutes before 10 PM. Rain was pouring down and I sat quietly for a few minutes watching the flickering light of the TV through the window. That whole night, nothing felt right. Every intimacy we ever shared, from dancing to *Stairway to Heaven* to our first kiss after *Star Wars* to our Prom night brought us progressively closer. What we did on this night did not.

I knocked quietly on the door, not wanting to wake up the kids Dawn was watching if they were already asleep. Dawn answered immediately, as if she had been standing by the door waiting for me. Her earlier bravado on the phone was missing. She looked like what she was–a young girl who was feeling unsure of herself.

"Hi, baby. Are the kids asleep?"

"Mmm-hmm. Come on in."

The television was tuned to Dick Clark's New Year's Rockin' Eve. That and the raindrops beating down would be the soundtrack to our first time. We sat on the couch and tried to talk, but we knew this night wasn't about talking. Eventually I worked my courage up and pulled her close to me. I strongly sensed that we were making a mistake, but that didn't slow me down.

At one point, I looked over Dawn's shoulder and saw that Chuck Mangione was on the TV, playing *Feels So Good*. The irony was lost on me at the time.

I walked out of the house before 11:00 PM. I had thought I would feel exhilarated, but all I felt was sadness. I strongly felt that I had a made a mistake. As the older one in the relationship, I should have been stronger.

While I had been inside, the weather had turned worse, with wind gusts added to the sleeting rain. I wasn't ready to go home. I definitely didn't want to face questions from Mom about why I was home before midnight on New Year's Eve. I started the car, turned the defroster on and eventually realized I was driving to St. Ives church outside of town.

I parked the car and went around the church to the graveyard in back. St. Ives sat in a bucolic spot, right next to a lake, but on this night it was filled with odd shadows and sounds. I ignored the driving rain and got out of the Vega and knelt in the wet, muddy grass beside my Dad's grave. I ignored the driving wind and rain and put my hand on the headstone and talked to my dad.

"Dad, I think I blew it. I love her, and I never thought being with her could be wrong, but it was. I can't stand that I let this happen. What can I do to make it right?"

The wind rose and I shouted over it, ignoring the spattering rain and freezing cold.

"I can't undo what I did tonight, but if I can, I'll make it right, I swear." I was hoping to hear back from him, but after what felt like a very long silence, I went back to the sanctuary of the car. I turned my headlights on. The headstones looked eerie in the pouring rain, illuminated by my lights and casting crazy shadows everywhere.

I felt spent in every way. I drove home slowly to Damron Road. I don't know how long I was at the graveyard, but when I walked into the darkened house, dripping wet, the clock on top of the television said it was 1:30 in the morning.

1979 had arrived.

More Than a Feeling

The New Year dawned without time to ponder what had happened the night before. I had to get on the road early to pick up my friend at Sea-Tac airport and return his car to him. I didn't see Dawn at all that day. If I had, I didn't have the communication skills to express the complex thoughts and feelings running through me. I was more in love with Dawn than ever, and in the clear light of morning, my time kneeling and crying at Dad's grave seemed melodramatic.

As I put more miles between me and Mossyrock, my fears decreased. I reminded myself that only Dawn and I knew we had been together, and neither of us was talking. We had made it through the Christmas holiday unscathed, and we would be able to keep seeing each other.

I didn't see Dawn at all in January. I funneled all my money into buying parts so I could get the Vega back on the road. Also, Dawn and I wanted to show Colleen we weren't going to abuse the privilege of seeing each other. I thought the best way to accomplish that was to make myself scarce around Mossyrock.

Finally, I needed to repair my grade point average. I had registered for a full schedule and I was determined to get better grades. With Dawn in my life again, I found myself focusing on the future.

Even though we were apart, we talked on the phone occasionally. Long distance was still an expensive luxury we couldn't afford, but we supplemented those short conversations with long letters.

I spent January studying the intricacies of Chaucer's

Canterbury Tales in Middle English and preparing for Speech and Debate classes. In the meantime, one of my roommates got the Vega running again after many hours of unpaid effort. I was no longer chained to my room.

Valentine's Day eventually appeared on the horizon. Through brief phone calls and longer letters, Dawn and I decided we would see each other then. It fell in the middle of the week, so we decided to celebrate the weekend before. I would drive down and watch Dawn play in her volleyball game at Morton on Friday night. We would spend as much time together as we thought we could get away with that weekend before I departed late Sunday afternoon.

The Thursday night before I was supposed to leave for the Rock, I was on a studying jag. I was attempting to get an entire weekend's homework done in one night. It was getting late, and I was in the middle of writing an essay about the symbolism in *Sir Gawain and the Green Knight* when my landlord shouted downstairs that I had a phone call. I climbed the stairs, picked up the phone. "Hello?"

I was met with a hurricane of screaming and obscenities. It changed my life forever.

After listening to a steady torrent of abuse for thirty seconds, I figured out it was Dawn's dad, Walt, on the other end. I couldn't make out what he was saying. He was too upset to enunciate.

"Walt. I can't understand you," I said. "What's wrong?"

He wouldn't stop screaming. It was like yelling into gale force winds. Finally, with an exasperated howl, I heard him slam the phone down on a table. I didn't know what was happening, but my insides were congealing.

I held the phone to my ear, waiting for the silence to be broken. A few seconds later, I heard Colleen's voice on the line. Her tone was deadly calm.

"Shawn? I have to apologize for my husband. He's

upset. So am I." Her voice was so calm that she didn't sound upset at all.

"Okay, just tell me what's wrong."

"Shawn," Colleen said. "We know you had sex with Dawn. Now, we need you to know Dawn is pregnant. And, before you get any ideas about what's going to happen next, I need you to know you will never see our daughter again. We have already scheduled an abortion, which will cost $400, and you will pay for that. In exchange for that and never seeing Dawn again, we will not press statutory rape charges against you."

It was way more information than I could absorb.

They knew Dawn and I had been together. That was bad.

Dawn was pregnant. That was mega-bad.

She had said, "We've already scheduled an abortion." I couldn't begin to wrap my mind around that idea. There was too much pain there. The phone was silent for what seemed like an eternity.

"I... I'm sorry," I said limply. "I know how wrong it was for Dawn and me to have been together. It was my fault. I messed up."

"Yes, you did."

I said that Dawn wasn't the only one to lose her innocence that night. She blasted back at me, saying it wasn't her fault I was a bathroom idiot. It took me a while after the phone call to understand what she meant.

"Please don't schedule an abortion, I'll do anything," I pleaded with her. "My sister can help me pay for all of Dawn's medical expenses. Even if she has the baby and gives it up for adoption that would be so much better."

"Shawn, Dawn is fifteen years old. We will not allow her to have a baby." I felt like I had wandered onstage in a play where everyone but me already knew their lines.

I told her I would quit school immediately and get a job to support her. That finally cut through her calm demeanor and she snapped at me.

"We know you *want* to marry Dawn, but don't you get it?"

"What?"

"You've ruined Dawn's life. She never wants to see you again."

I was stunned. How could that be?

Colleen repeated herself and I stood motionless. The more I thought about it, the more sense it made. I ruined her life. Of course she didn't want to see me again.

I didn't want to give up. But no matter what I said, she came back to the same two options: give her $400 and promise never to see Dawn again, or face criminal charges. I wasn't willing to accept either, so I told them I was driving down to meet with them face-to-face.

Colleen agreed to meet me Saturday afternoon at their house, but left me with a final warning.

"We'll meet with you," she said. "But these options won't change." Her words rang in my ears after I hung up the phone. I was numb. I stumbled down the stairs and sat on my bed, waiting for my brain to kick into gear. I sat on my bed with my back, fittingly, against the wall. No matter how hard I tried, I couldn't digest Colleen's words. I found only darkness and despair at the end of every thought. I was only nineteen, but I felt old and wasted.

I could handle not seeing Dawn again for a long time. I'd been training for that. It would be horrible to lose her again so soon after getting her back in my life, but I could handle it. The idea that Dawn was pregnant and Walt and Colleen were going to force her to abort the baby was something I could not begin to accept.

Before I left for Mossyrock that morning, I drove to Auburn to meet with Terri. I poured my heart out to her and told her the whole story. Terri wanted to go to her bank, take out $5000, give it to Walt and Colleen, and tell them that would cover the baby's birth.

I wouldn't let her do it. I knew it wouldn't work. I believed this situation had presented Walt and Colleen with a final solution to the problem of me being with their daughter. I did ask to borrow the $400, so when I met with them I would have all options open.

My final stop before Mossyrock was the small town of Salkum, where my former newspaper advisor and English teacher Jim Bartee lived. After listening to my tale of woe, Jim berated me for putting myself and Dawn into this situation. Eventually, he saw I was already as low as a human being can be, and he agreed to go with me the next day to meet with Walt and Colleen.

I needed to find Dawn. Her feelings would strongly influence how I would respond to the choices Walt and Colleen gave me. I decided to drive to Morton to watch Dawn play her volleyball game. That might be my only chance to talk to her before the confrontation with her parents.

As I walked into the Morton gym, my stomach knotted with the anticipation and dread. I had no idea what her reaction would be. Would she be afraid to talk to me in public? Would she even want to talk to me? Did she hate me already for getting her pregnant? Could she still love me?

I found a spot on the sidelines where I thought I might be able to catch Dawn's eye during the game. She was already on the floor when I sat down. She spotted me within a minute of my arrival, just in time to miss an easy dig.

The match ended in less than an hour with a victory for the hated Morton Huskies. I didn't care. I stood outside the locker room in the most obvious spot I could, hoping to catch Dawn before she boarded the team bus. Right on schedule, she came through the double doors and made her way straight to me. She was so scared and nervous I felt like I was talking to a complete stranger.

"How are you?" I asked. I had never meant that question more. I really needed to know. Her expression was completely blank, but with a hint of fear hiding underneath. She shrugged and looked around anxiously.

"Baby, I really need to talk to you," I said.

"I don't know how we can. I've got to go."

It happened so fast. I'd had a plan. I was going to go up to her and hold her and tell her how sorry I was I had put us in that situation. I loved her more than anything in the world and I would do anything to save our baby. I rehearsed it on the drive down from Seattle. But when the moment arrived, I was frozen and helpless. I was paralyzed by her anxiety and fear. I stood motionless while she boarded the team bus. I imagined her staring out through one of the darkened windows while I watched. I stood there until the bus slowly pulled away and watched it cruise slowly into the night.

I drove silently home from Morton, slipped into the quiet trailer, and spent another sleepless night in my childhood bed. It was the same place I had spent so many nights before, dreaming of Dawn Adele.

Seeing her so freighted by nerves and fear clarified the harm I was causing her. The worst thing was that it was entirely my fault. I knew Dawn had no chance for a normal high school life as long as I was in it. I wanted her to have football games and dances and fun with all of her friends. I didn't want her to have to jump at shadows. I loved her too much to think of her throwing everything away for an endless series of clandestine meetings. I'd already had my happy high school days. I knew I couldn't ask Dawn to go straight from adolescence to adult responsibility.

I finally had the answer to the question I had posed to myself in my poem to her, *Where Can I Find the Strength*.

Which will finally prove the stronger/my need for you/or my desire for your best?

I was ashamed by how long it took me to reach the answer.

Late Saturday morning, after my second consecutive sleepless night, I sat on my front porch waiting for Jim Bartee. Right on schedule, Jim's silver Volvo with the bumper sticker, *One World, One Faith* pulled into my driveway. It felt like my world was coming to an end, but I knew it was important to have Jim there.

Jim knocked on the door and Walt let us into the living room. Walt and Colleen sat in their usual places while Jim and I sat in two chairs that had been moved to the far end of the living room. Dawn stood next to the wood stove, with tears in her eyes but unable to look at me. There was a stiff and formal air to the room like an arraignment. It turned out to be more like a sentencing.

Walt and Colleen passed their final judgment and I forced myself to my feet. I asked Colleen if I could say goodbye to Dawn. She said that was fine. We moved as far away as we could get, but still stood within easy earshot of Walt, Colleen and Jim.

"You know I'll still love you when we can see each other again, right?"

I wanted to grab her hand but I could feel Colleen staring at us.

"Do you... remember *I Will Still Love You?*" Dawn's voice was choked by her tears. I could barely understand what she was saying.

"The song by Stonebolt?"

She nodded and looked down.

I couldn't speak any more either. My throat was so tight it hurt. Tears ran down both our faces without stopping. I didn't want to leave her, but I couldn't stand the feeling of impending doom. I kissed her softly on the cheek and walked out the door, Jim trailing behind me.

When we got back to his Volvo, Jim said, "I counted your tears, and they were the perfect number. There was not too many or too few."

I nodded, although I had no idea what that meant. I thanked him again for being there. He got in his car and drove off.

I would only talk to Dawn one more time until December 1st, 2006.

Oh, and that song that Dawn asked me to remember? That was an odd song to bring up at that moment. Music was so important to us, and we had so many songs we thought of as ours. Oddly enough, *I Will Still Love You* had never been one of them. I listened to the lyrics of that song hundreds of times over the next few years, trying to decipher the last message she gave me. The song talks about leaving your lover, finding your own way in life, and then returning to each other. As I got into my car and drove back to Seattle, I could only hope that was what lay ahead for us.

Lost Without Your Love

Nearly three years passed between the day I said my last goodbye to Dawn and her 18th birthday. I thought about her nearly every day with the same intensity as the day I said goodbye, but I had to get on with life. The obstacles I had with the opposite sex slowly evaporated, and I went out with a series of women. It was easier because I didn't care. The less I cared, the easier it was to find women who would go out with me. A guy with a broken heart is a fixer-upper most women can't resist.

I loved Dawn, and I knew no one would ever equal her in my life. I was confident our years of exile would pass and we would eventually be together. I still imagined that we would get married, have kids, and grow old together.

I decided not to go back to the University of Washington for spring quarter. It felt like that was too tied up with the future I had planned for Dawn and me. Even though she had never so much as stepped foot on the UW, it had felt like I carried her with me to every class. Just walking onto the campus again was painful.

Still, I had to do something with my life, so I enrolled in The Ron Bailie School of Broadcast, located at 2nd and Denny in downtown Seattle. I graduated in February 1980. My first full-time gig in radio was at KHDN in Hardin, Montana, "The Zucchini Capital of the World." It was every bit as exciting as the name suggested.

After I'd spent six months in Hardin, KHDN went broke. I ended up back in Seattle, which is where I was living during Christmas 1981. The economy was in the tank by then. Most of my family was unemployed and so broke that we didn't have money to buy each other presents. Instead we agreed to re-gift items we already had, or give homemade gifts.

Dawn was set to turn eighteen two days after Christmas, and I would be released from the prison of waiting for her. I drove to Mossyrock on Christmas Eve. I brought the engagement ring that I had bought years before. I wanted her to know she had never been outside my heart.

I also brought a birthday present for Dawn. I talked a friend of mine, who specialized in calligraphy, into writing a phrase on heavy card stock. It read,

Let I, Who am a Part of God,
Find the Part of Me that Is a Part of You.

I matted it so it was ready to hang on the wall. That's how I felt when I was with her–like we created something sacred.

I hadn't even seen a glimpse of Dawn next door by the time her birthday arrived. At 8 PM that night, Mom, Dad, Terri, Tommy and I were in the living room watching a movie. My eyes constantly strayed over to Dawn's house. Finally, I couldn't take it anymore. I slipped into the kitchen. Even though it was still four hours until Dawn's 18th birthday, I couldn't wait any longer. We had done the time for our crimes. I knew I could finally call her, after three years of waiting.

I had pictured this moment in my head thousands of times. It was finally here. My hand trembled as I picked up the phone. I dialed Dawn's number from memory. Walt answered after a few rings.

"Walt, this is Shawn. Can I speak to Dawn please?"

He didn't answer me. I heard the clunk of the receiver hitting a table. I thought of the anger and recriminations I heard the last time I spoke to Walt on the phone three years earlier. At least he didn't scream at me before throwing the phone down this time. After a long wait, I heard Dawn's voice.

"Hello?" Her voice was so tight and unnatural that I barely recognized it.

"Dawn, it's Shawn." I paused nervously and listened. There was no response. "I was wondering if you want to meet me out in the yard so we could talk."

I had spent a lot of time thinking about exactly what I would say when I could finally talk to Dawn again. This seemed like the best choice. I liked the symmetry of meeting in the same spot where we had shared our first kiss and spent so many happy hours together. This all depended on one key element that I hadn't considered; whether Dawn might want to talk to me.

"I don't think so," she said. Her voice was hollow, and I heard a sense of finality.

My heart broke.

"You don't think so," I repeated.

I heard her exhale, and the distant sound of TV in the background.

"Okay then. Bye." I hung up. There wasn't anything else to do. I felt the vinyl of Mom's kitchen chair under me and realized I had sat down. I had been waiting for this moment for so long. Now that it had come and gone so fruitlessly, I didn't know what to do.

I waited for my world to start spinning again. Without knowing where I was going, I was on my feet and moving. In the living room, the rest of my family was still watching the movie. I walked numbly back to my childhood bedroom and picked up my UW backpack with Dawn's birthday present. Without telling anyone I was going, I slipped out the back door, walked out to my car and started it quietly.

I stared through the frozen windshield at Dawn's room, waiting to see if the light would come on. It stayed dark. I felt like someone had knocked the wind out of me, and I wondered if she felt the same.

I slipped my car into reverse, backed onto Damron Road, and headed for Seattle. I replayed our conversation over and over in my head as I drove.

Somewhere between Centralia and Olympia, I realized I still had the little blue box with the engagement ring in my coat pocket. I rolled my window down and frigid air filled the car. I took one last look at the rings, framing them in my memory. I threw it as far out the window as I could. I was doing better than seventy miles per hour and never saw them again.

As 1982 wore on, I began to think that the cold December night when Dawn spurned me was some sort of mistake. Maybe I had caught her off guard, calling her out of the blue after three years.

By August, I was ready to try again. I drove to Mossyrock. Calling her out of the blue hadn't worked out too well, so I thought I needed another plan. Eventually, I decided to send her flowers. I called a florist and ordered three roses to be delivered to her—one for each year we had been apart. I asked them to include a card that read, "I'm next door if you want to talk - Shawn." My hope was that this time she would gather her thoughts before we talked, and maybe I'd get a different reaction.

I nervously watched the florist come and go at her front door. I fantasized about Dawn rushing across the yard and bounding up the steps like she used to do. But hours passed and nothing happened.

Finally, late that evening I heard my step-dad holler at me to come to the front door. I was hoping to see Dawn. Instead, it was Rick Johnson, a kid in Dawn's class. He was holding the roses at his hip and looked pissed.

We stood staring at each other across the threshold of the front door. It took me a few moments to realize that Dawn had a boyfriend, and he was here to make a point. I walked outside to talk to Rick. He pushed the flowers in my chest.

"Look. I don't want you bothering Dawn any more. She doesn't want to see you."

"Well, if that's the way she feels, then I won't try to talk to her any more. But, you know Dawn and I have a history together and there are some things I wanted to talk to her about. Still, if I had known she had a boyfriend, I never would have sent her the flowers. I don't want to upset Dawn. Tell her I'll never talk to her again if that's what she wants."

"I'm telling you to never talk to her again."

He was getting more agitated and aggressive now. He wasn't very big, but the last thing I wanted to do was get in a fight with Dawn's boyfriend in my parents front yard.

"Will you just give her that message please? If she doesn't want to talk to me, I'll never bother her again."

He didn't answer me, but just shook his head, spit on the ground and walked away.

I kept my end of the bargain. I didn't see Dawn again for twenty five years.

Please Don't Let Me Be Misunderstood

On January 5th, 2007, I took the day off to drive to Longview and collect the rent on some duplexes I owned. It was the same thing I'd been doing the month before when I had run into Dawn at Bill & Bea's. Collecting the rents was my excuse for the trip, but I was really hoping to see her again.

It was early afternoon when I passed through Centralia. I pulled hopefully into the Bill & Bea's drive-thru lane, but I saw right away that Dawn wasn't there. I recognized her daughter, Connie, and I think she recognized me, but neither of us said anything.

By the time I made it to Longview and collected the rents, it was getting late. When I pulled off at the last Centralia exit on the way back to Enumclaw, it was almost closing time at Bill & Bea's. As soon as I pulled up to the drive-thru, I saw Dawn. My heart rate skyrocketed. Just like last time, it seemed to take each car in front of me forever to get their order.

When I finally pulled up to the window, I looked for a glimmer of recognition. Nothing. I grasped for something to say, hoping for something smooth or at least comprehensible. Instead, I thought back to our meeting a month earlier.

"You're not going to freak out on me again, are you?" I asked. It wasn't the best opening line.

"No," she said coldly. "I'm over that now."

Dawn can do so much damage to me with so few

words. In 1981, when I asked to meet her in the yard, she said four words: "I don't think so." Tonight, it was "I'm over that now."

"Can I take your order?" she asked. I chuckled nervously, hoping she was joking and this was her way of shrugging off her overreaction of the previous month.

She glared silently at me.

I couldn't think of anything intelligent to say, so I ordered a chicken sandwich that I knew I would never be able to eat. I watched as she helped a customer at the counter, smiling and being kind to him.

After a few minutes, she brought my order to the window, took my money, and handed me the bag with my order in it.

"It was great to see you again, Dawn."

"You too."

I knew she didn't mean that in any way. She turned toward the counter and her other customers. I drove away blindly, certain I had blown it again, sure that had been my final opportunity.

Against the Wind

I closed the front door behind me, slipped my headphones on, and stepped off my front porch with Jenny leaping ahead of me. At home, she was never more than a few feet from me. At night, when I took her for a walk, she liked to run ahead of me, her feather-duster tail sweeping the air behind her. Jenny was originally for my girls when I brought her home from the pound, but everyone knew she was my dog.

That first day of June 2009 was unusually warm. The ten o'clock news said the high temperature was 83, and it was still warm outside. I worked up a sweat walking Jenny to the end of the street and back.

My malaise had only grown more pronounced over the previous three years. I was still unable to extricate myself from my unhappy marriage to Adinah. There had never been much intimacy in our marriage, but whatever little there had been was long since gone.

We had spent more than two years in counseling, but I had no intention of making progress. I was trying to find the most comfortable way I could to end the marriage so I could live peacefully alone. I had arranged a private session with our marriage counselor a few days earlier. After so many fruitless sessions, I finally told her the truth about how I felt about my marriage. At the end of that meeting, she said she didn't need to struggle any more to save the marriage. Those few words lifted a massive weight off me.

Also, I was a real estate broker. It was a career that had afforded me a comfortable lifestyle for fifteen years.

But since the real estate market crash in 2007, the joy had evaporated. In 2009, I earned less than half what I had made just three years earlier.

Most importantly, in the last six months I had lost the two people I was closest to. My nephew Tommy, who had shared so many lifetime adventures with me, passed away from liver failure in December. He was a lifelong alcoholic, and in the end, it caught up to him fast. He lapsed into a coma in California and died before I could get down to see him one last time.

Two days after Tommy died, his mom, Terri, died of a massive heart attack. Losing Tommy was more than she could bear. She was eighteen years older than me and was always more like a mom than a big sister. She was also my best friend for most of my adult life. I trusted Terri with my innermost thoughts. Now there was no one left to trust.

Both my mom and step-dad had passed away in the last three years. It was starting to feel like there was no one left, and that was not a good feeling.

I looked forward to the fifteen minutes each night when I walked Jenny because it was my only time to be completely alone. I crossed Bondgard Avenue and walked along the empty lots Jenny loved to explore. I turned up the volume on Boston's *More Than a Feeling* on my iPod.

We walked to the dead end of the road and she sniffed around the retaining pond. I climbed up a small hill of dirt the builders had left on the last vacant lot, turned toward Mt. Peak, and looked beyond it. Facing south toward Centralia, I relaxed my mind and let thoughts of Dawn wash over me. I hadn't seen or spoken to her since the night she had been so cold to me two and a half years before. A normal person would have forgotten her and gotten on with life. She lived in my thoughts every single day.

Things had been better when Terri was alive. I had

talked to her about Dawn and she understood. She listened, asked questions, and cared. In early December 2008, Terri called me with an unusual request.

"Little brother, I need a favor."

Terri had done me more favors in my lifetime than I could count, so I didn't hesitate.

"Name it, and it's yours."

"I want you to publish your story with Dawn."

I had already written the story and sent it to her, but I had done so to get some feedback and perspective.

"Now why do you want to ask me to do something like that? That's private. It's personal."

"It's too late. You already promised."

I agreed to try and find a way to get it published someday and quickly forgot about it. Two weeks later, Terri was dead. In a moment, that promise became a vow I would do anything in my power to fulfill. I went online and looked for a website that accepted submissions from unpublished authors. Getting my story published seemed daunting, and I had no idea where to begin. My first search took me to a website called WritingRaw.com. I spent a few hours reading the stories there and liked what I saw.

I took a chance and sent off the first chapter of my story to Weeb Heinrich, who ran WritingRaw.com. I was surprised when I got a quick response, telling me he liked my story and that he would publish it on the site within 24 hours.

I wanted to write the story as a serial and send off a new chapter every other week. Weeb was open to that idea and it gave me incentive to keep writing. I hoped that writing and publishing the story might finally exorcise the demons I had carried inside for thirty years. But it wasn't that simple, and here I was staring southward toward Centralia thinking about Dawn.

A year earlier I had tried to reach her one last time.

She joined Classmates.com, and I sent her an email hoping to inspire a conversation.

> *Dawn,*
>
> *I'm sure it seems a little out of the blue to get an email from me, but I would like to have a chance to talk with you. I'd like to see if we could be friends. When I left you in 1979, I was counting the days until I could talk to you again, and now over 10,000 days have passed and we haven't had a single conversation. That seems wrong to me.*
>
> *I don't have any way of knowing where you are in your life right now, but I'd like to catch up with you. It's possible you're happy with not having spoken to me for the last thirty years. I wasn't sure if your first reaction at seeing me again was happiness, horror, or just shock, but I admit it was a little deflating when you looked at me and said, "Shawn who?!"*
>
> *I would like to get to know you again, but if you don't have an interest in that, just drop me a line and let me know, and that'll be that. I agreed not to see you until you were 18 all those years ago because I thought that was what was best for you. My regret now is that I didn't talk to you about that decision. That was wrong, and I'm sorry.*
>
> *I hope to hear from you...*
> *Shawn*

Like every other time I tried to contact her for the last three decades, it was a dead end. I never heard from her.

Now I was looking out toward Centralia while Jenny sniffed the dirt. *More Than a Feeling* was playing on a continuous loop in my ears and it emboldened me. I focused all my energy toward Dawn, holding a perfect vision of her in my mind.

Dawn. Please. Come to me. Find me. I repeated this thought over and over, putting my entire being into it. I don't know how long I stood on the dirt pile, but I looked down to see that Jenny was eyeing me curiously. I climbed down the hill and patted Jenny on the head because she was such a good girl. I walked slowly back to the house.

I went upstairs, climbed into bed and lay listening to the crickets serenading me through my open window. I was asleep in less than five minutes and had an exceedingly strange dream. I had dreamed about Dawn ever since we had parted. Those dreams always stayed with me for a few days. Sometimes, it felt like I had actually been with her. Those dreams would leave a hole in me every time, stirring up all the old feelings–longing, pain, love, guilt, and regret.

They always had a similar theme. Dawn and I were close to each other, but not allowed to talk. The settings of the dreams changed, but the theme of separation lived in each of them. In three decades worth of dreams, we never had a conversation.

I dreamed of her again on this night. We were back in Mossyrock. I was standing on one side of the fence my step-dad had built and Dawn was on the other. As always in my dreams, she acted as if she couldn't talk to me. However, this time she gestured for me to follow her as she walked away. By the time I got around the fence she was gone, but I could see her standing inside her old bedroom. She was at the window, looking at me and smiling. It had been so many years since she had smiled at me–even in a dream–that it warmed me clear through. She remained silent as I approached the window. She pointed to a bulletin board on her wall. There were pictures of the people she had known and loved over her lifetime in the shape of a circle. The middle of the circle was empty, except for a picture of us. She pointed at the picture, looked at me and smiled again.

I woke up early the next morning thinking about the dream. While I had slept, my subconscious mind had given me the first poem I'd written in almost thirty years:

gone for so many years
alive in my dreams
hidden from the world
safe in my heart
now you are here
not a dream
in my sight
awakening me
if you touch me
in this harsh world
let me fall into your eyes
who would I dream of then?

Despite the poem, the thought of magically summoning Dawn into my life was a distant memory. I left the house before anyone else was awake and sat down at my desk to check my email. In my inbox was an email that had been sent at 10:14 the night before. There was no subject, but the sender was Dawn Johnson.

Time Passages

An hour passed after seeing Dawn's name in my inbox, and I still hadn't read her email. I had dreamed about being in contact with her for thirty years, but it had never happened. I hadn't heard so much as a whisper from Dawn for all those years.

Now, with her name staring back at me unblinking from my Hotmail account, I thought about how badly I missed Terri. If she had still been alive, I would have called her and read the email aloud to her. She would have understood and supported me. She was gone, though, and I was on my own. I steeled myself for the rejection I was sure was coming and opened the email.

Well, hello.

I don't know if I am fated to contact you or what. I logged into Classmates.com and saw the message you sent how long ago? I haven't been there since I signed up over a year ago. Then Connie, the daughter you met, called me to let me know some odd dude wrote a story about me and you can find it if you Google Bill & Bea's. I was mortified. My daughter now knows that "my first" is still in love with me.

I'm happy, in love, and my two daughters are happy. I am a supervisor for Verizon Wireless customer service, which means I get called terrible names all day, every day. The only difference between that and my marriage is that now I get paid for it.

Sorry I didn't recognize you at Bill and Bea's. I was what, 15 when I saw you last? I don't remember a lot of that time. In your message you asked if we can be friends. Well, there's no such thing as too many friends. However, my daughter thinks you are odd. I wonder myself.

Dawn

I re-read it three times, trying to absorb it. Most people would interpret her email as a punch in the gut. I was oddly exhilarated. There were a lot of negatives, including saying she was mortified by the story I had written that had somehow found its way into her hands, and that she thought I was odd. But then again, I am odd. I couldn't dispute that. I focused on two things. She wondered if she was fated to contact me, and she seemed to leave the door open to possible friendship. Those two things put me closer to having a real conversation with her than I had been in thirty years.

It struck me what a fantastic chain of coincidences had conspired to result in that email. The odds were incredible that Dawn's daughter would stumble across my story on WritingRaw.com, especially eighteen months after I had met her, but it happened. To have that happen at the same time Dawn logged back into Classmates.com seemed like the hand of Fate. It also felt like this chance to talk with my lifetime mystery girl could disappear at any moment, so I wrote her back immediately.

Hello Dawn,

First, let me apologize for the fact that your daughter stumbled across that story online. I thought I had changed enough information so it wouldn't pop up on a Google search. Obviously, I was wrong. I really am sorry. It was never my intent for anyone you know to see it and embarrass you. I contacted the site where the chapters were posted to have them taken down. They're already gone, so nobody will accidentally run across them again. Anyway, please accept my apology for any embarrassment I may have caused you.

In your email, you said that you were in love, and I'm glad for you. When I knew you thirty years ago, I thought you were the best person I had ever met. You deserve happiness, and that's what I hope you find.

I know that you said in your email that you don't remember much of anything from that time, but there are a couple of things that I would like to talk to you about. Would you mind answering a few questions some time?

I hope that everything is good with you and that we can be friends going forward. It was good hearing from you...

Shawn

I wasn't quite as thrilled as I claimed that she was in love with someone. Above all, I hoped to find the answers to questions I'd been hauling like excess baggage for too many years.

Before I left for lunch another email appeared.

I will help answer questions you have. My memory of faces is lousy, but I think I remember just about everything else.

Yes, I am in love. I married Rick Johnson a few years out of high school. We were together up until a few years ago. Drugs became a major factor in his life and I finally had enough. I am now with someone who thinks I am beautiful. We have been together for a couple of years and I am

very happy.
It is good to hear from you.
Dawn

Two emails from her in the same day, and in both of them she said how in love and happy she was. I was sure she was saying that to keep me at arm's distance, since she knew how I felt about her from reading the story online. But, it was also possible that she maybe didn't feel as happy and contented in her relationship as she said.

I zipped off a quick email asking her whether she remembered getting that crazy letter I sent her from Long Beach all those years ago. I was curious about that, but I also wanted to get her thinking about our happy times together and see how much she remembered.

I went out to lunch, and by the time I got back there was another email waiting for me.

I remember that letter. What I remember
most about it is that in the letter you said that you
were finally going to say you loved me out loud.
But, it wasn't out loud. It was in a letter. My mom
read that and laughed. I miss her. My dad died a
few years ago too, so they're both gone.

I don't remember talking about the letter
with you. I wouldn't have, though. I would have
been too embarrassed. It was the first time a boy
told me they loved me. However, I also remember
that not only my mom read it, but all the girls at a
sleep over read it too. You know how girls are.
Dawn

I wouldn't have thought I could be embarrassed by something that happened more than thirty years ago, but the thought of Dawn and her teenage friends laying around on sleeping bags and reading that letter did it.

That's what I got for sending a love letter to a girl so young. Before I left work that night I sent off one last response.

Dawn

When I thought about you having a sleepover and reading that letter to the other girls, it was my turn to be mortified. It would have killed me at the time, but now it seems funny.

I'm glad to know you got that letter. Since we never talked about it, I had begun to wonder if it was real or if I had imagined writing it. Of course, Colleen was right. It was silly for me to write a letter to you and say that I wanted to say it "out loud." I didn't know what to do with everything I was feeling for you, so I did what I always did—I wrote. In fact, that's why I am writing the story I am now, to help me figure out some things from when we were together that are still impacting me today.

You mention missing Colleen. As badly as things ended between us, I've thought of her often as well. I was on the air in Greybull Wyoming when Mom called to tell me she had passed away. I wanted to call you then to tell you I was sorry, but I thought you didn't want to hear from me. I would have liked to talk to her again, although I don't think she felt the same about me. In the years before you and I were together, I had come to think of Colleen as my friend. I can tell you now that I am sorry she passed away. It's so hard when our parents leave us. You know my Dad died when I was little, and now Mom and Robert both passed away a few years ago too.

Shawn

That night, as I walked Jenny, I stood on my little dirt hill and again looked to the south. I was humbled and amazed that Dawn had found me, and that I was actually talking to her.

When I walked back in the house I knew I would have to talk with Adinah about being in contact with Dawn. As good as I was at hiding my emotions, this was too much to hide. I told her I needed to talk to her and she tensed up. We'd been in marriage counseling for two years and we both knew a conversation that started with 'I need to talk to you' could go anywhere.

"I want to tell you that I've been exchanging emails with Dawn today."

I didn't need to explain who Dawn was. I had told Adinah when I ran into Dawn at Bill & Bea's in 2006. She had hovered over our marriage ever since. We didn't talk about her often, but when we did, it was always a highly charged conversation. I was always factually truthful with Adinah but I was emotionally dishonest. I couldn't begin to tell her how I really felt.

"Is that so?" she asked. "What did you talk about?"

"Honestly, not too much. But there are a couple of things I need to tell you. One is that I was so blown away when I first ran into Dawn a few years ago. I sat down and wrote out the story of when we were together. It turned out to be a lot longer than I had thought it would be, something like a book."

"Well that's just great, isn't it?" She folded her arms. "You're married to me, but you're writing a book about some girl you haven't talked to in thirty years?"

"Not my finest moment, I know."

"I guess not."

"Look, I'm tired of dishonesty. That's why I'm telling you this. I doubt if you want to read it, but if you do, there's a copy in my closet."

"I couldn't care less about your stupid story."

"I understand why you feel that way, but I wanted to tell you about it. And, there's one more thing I need you to know. I'm not going to stop talking to her. I'm not going to sneak around behind your back about anything."

"Really."

"Yeah. I don't know if I'll talk to her for a few days or a week or forever, but I'm gonna talk to her some more." I hoped that Adinah would balk at that but she didn't.

"Fine, I don't care. Do what you need to do."

Reminiscing

I was in an odd place with Dawn. She had read the story I had posted online, so she knew I loved her after so many years. I would never deny those feelings, but we didn't talk about them either. I didn't want to put Dawn into the position of having to reject me outright. We ignored that elephant in the room and got to know each other again.

In those first emails, we talked a lot about the past, comparing notes about our memories of being together. I was happy and relieved to find our memories agreed on most things, even though there were things that Dawn remembered with clarity that I didn't, and vice versa.

Over the next few weeks, we found ourselves sending more emails every day. At first it was a couple each day, then three or four, and eventually we were in constant contact. You might think that meant we were growing closer and more intimate, but it didn't feel that way. Over those first few weeks of June, Dawn seemed wary of me, like I was a stranger. After thirty years, I guess I was.

Eventually we started to catch up with what our lives had been like over the past few years. I told her about my first marriage and how much it hurt when my first wife left and took my three girls to Arkansas. My first wife leaving me was a blessing, but losing Desi, Samy and Sabrina to Arkansas almost killed me.

In return, Dawn told me about her marriage, to the same Rick Johnson who once returned the roses I sent her all those years ago:

My marriage with Rick was pretty bad. For the longest time, I thought I was going crazy. Then, one night a neighbor called the police. That was the night I found out that he was doing meth. That answered a lot of questions and made the past few years make a lot more sense. He tried to quit, I tried to stay with him. It didn't work.

Dawn

Dawn and Rick had been separated for years but still hadn't gotten divorced. Dawn said she was afraid to file the papers. Divorce is expensive and money was tight for her. I had a feeling that she used the fact that she was still married as a barrier to keep anyone she was seeing from getting too close.

After several weeks of emails, I was thrilled to be in touch with Dawn. But I was getting nowhere on the central mysteries that had bothered me for decades. What happened to her after we separated? Had she really been pregnant? Why had she rejected any communication with me for so long, but now was willing to talk? I got my first clue to those questions two weeks after our first email, when Dawn wrote:

I did have anger toward you. I was very young when we were together and I saw you as a manipulative older guy who talked me into things. I thought for the longest time you had ruined my life. I suppose it was easy to think that because you were gone and Mom was always telling me that.

It wasn't until my daughter Dani became pregnant at 16 that I realized that it didn't really happen the way I remembered it. Dani's boyfriend is 19, but she is the boss of that relationship. Over the years I have figured out

that most 18-19 year old boys are not very bright.
That is why I don't blame you for anything
anymore. It's easy for me to blame you for
everything, but it's a waste of time.
    Dawn

That felt like the beginning of an explanation. Those
words hurt because she was expressing why I always felt
guilty. I was older and should have controlled things better
than I did. But it was ironic that she went through life
blaming me for manipulating her, when our only time
together was initiated by her phone call. I didn't call her on
that because it felt like more disclosures were coming and I
didn't want to stop the flow of words.

When we first started talking again, I thought she had
read the whole story I had published on WritingRaw.com.
However, it turned out she had only found the first chapter,
which recounted our chance meeting at Bill & Bea's in 2006.
Ever since I had begun writing this story, I told myself it was
to get perspective and a better understanding of what
happened. Now, when there was a real chance that Dawn
would read what I had written, I knew that had been my
purpose all along. I wanted her to see how I felt about her
through my own eyes–how clear my memories of our time
together were. I sent her an email and asked if she would like
to read the rest of the story.

She said she would and I sent her a sample chapter. It
was the one where I took her to *Star Wars* for her birthday.
She lingered on one quote: *"I will almost certainly never*
know what Dawn was thinking or feeling as she went to
bed that night."

Soon after I sent her that chapter, I received this reply.

I'll tell you what I was thinking. At the time I
was thinking you were an older guy being nice to
me. You may have been just a teenager, but to me

you seemed a lot older. I was a kid still and too innocent for my own good. I was also in shock to find out that you had feelings for me. I really didn't know.

The night that you kissed me, I was trying to keep my knees from buckling. I felt the electricity the moment we kissed. I wouldn't have been able to speak if my life depended on it. I walked into my house and acted like everything was cool with my parents, like it was no big deal. I mumbled something to Mom and Dad then went straight to my room so I didn't have to talk any more. And I could remember that kiss.

Dawn

Finally, it felt like Dawn was letting me inside. She remembered our kiss, the one I had never been able to forget.

I wish I could say I waited long enough before responding, but I answered immediately.

I've spent a lot of time wondering why you stuck in my heart so firmly when every other person I've been with has left almost no impression at all. Do you remember when we would drive up to Doss Cemetery, turn the radio on softly, shuck off all our clothes and lay there and hold each other, skin to skin, but not do anything else? I sure never did anything like that again. During times like that, everyone says things like "I will always love you" and "I will never feel like this again." Then, time passes, things change, and we forget those things.

For me, time passed, but I never forgot those things. It was a life vow that I have kept sacred. Holding thoughts and feelings like that in my heart for 30 years has been detrimental to my other relationships. That may explain why the best relationships I've had in my life have been with my sister and daughters.

I found something with you–a level of trust and an emotional nakedness–that I never found again with another person.

Shawn

Less than an hour later, I heard from her again:

The time we were together was a very important time in my life. I have fond memories and some very sad memories that I blocked out just for my emotional survival. What we experienced was wonderful and terrible all at the same time. I would never want anyone else to go through what we went through. But, I don't regret any of it. I cherish it all, even the worst times. It was real. It was raw. It was not puppy love. I would have forgotten you a long time ago if it was.

What we had was so special that I haven't ever experienced anything like that again. I have been looking for it all this time. Whatever it is, I haven't found it. Is it because we had it? If that's the case, then how sad is that, having something people spend their whole lives looking for, but finding it oh so young.

Dawn

I was touched to finally get a peek behind the wall of silence that surrounded Dawn for so long. I could feel the warmth of the memories building in her words. I wrote back:

You blocked out the most painful stuff that

happened between us. That was why I left you in the first place. I was having a negative impact in your life, and I couldn't stand that. I thought the only way your life could get back to normal was if I was completely out of it. I never wanted to leave you, but it was the only integrity I could find in that horrible situation.

My biggest regret from that time was that I made that decision to leave you by myself. If I could, I would go back to that weekend and find a way to talk with you about it, so we could make that decision together. Even if we decided to do exactly the same thing, we would have made the decision together and I could live with it much easier today.

Shawn

I didn't hear from her the rest of the day and by the next morning I was wondering what her response would be. When I opened her first email of the day I was floored.

I am not feeling that great today. It might be because I am sleeping on the couch and it is one of the most uncomfortable couches ever. We are broken up, but I am staying there and sleeping on the couch until I can figure out where I am going to go.

Dawn.

And You, My Love

Everything was happening so fast. A month earlier, I had met with our marriage counselor to tell her I was throwing in the towel. Before I could share that with Adinah, Dawn appeared out of the blue, with a boyfriend and saying she was in love. A few weeks later, Dawn was unattached and sleeping on the couch. In the meantime, there was an inevitable conversation with Adinah coming, and I knew neither one of us was going to enjoy it.

Adinah had left for her annual summer trip to Arkansas and would be gone six weeks. I intended to sit down with her before she left and tell her our marriage was over. At the last minute, I realized that would delay her departure while we dealt with the fallout. I knew that was the right thing to do, but I took the cowardly way out. Once again, I chose to save that firestorm for another day.

After spending the previous eight years in a slow spiral, I wasn't going to complain. With Adinah gone, I had the freedom to let my mask of indifference slip away and be who I was. I was awake most of the night, replaying everything in my brain, trying to gain some perspective on the new developments in my life.

I had one of those crazy real estate days that left me with no time to think about anything else, and it was after 8 PM by the time I got home. I thought about writing Dawn another email, but that didn't seem like enough. I realized I needed to call her. It would be good to have a conversation where neither of us could read it over and edit our thoughts before sending. Several days earlier Dawn had sent me her phone number. I hadn't worked up the nerve to use it.

I went upstairs, set my iPod to play Chris Rea's *Road to Hell* album softly, and opened the window to let in a summer breeze. The frogs living behind the house were already in full voice. I entered her number but it went to voicemail. I tried to hide my disappointment as I left a message.

"Dawn, it's Shawn. It feels odd to be calling you after so many years. Anyway, I'm just home doing nothing and wanted to talk to you. Give me a call if you want to."

My phone rang less than five minutes later.

"Dawn?"

"Hi. I didn't recognize your number so I didn't answer."

"I figured. Are you still at work?"

"I'm at work, yeah. Am I working? No."

"Have you got time to talk or should I call you back?"

"No, this is good. What do you want to talk about?"

She sounded older than I remembered, of course. Her voice was throatier and I began the process of connecting this Dawn with the one I had held in my heart for so long.

I started talking. I told her about Desi, Samy, and Sabrina—who they are, what makes each of them special, and how much I love them. The first time I glanced over at the clock beside my bed I was surprised to see that I'd talked about my girls for almost an hour.

I asked Dawn about her girls and I heard pride in her voice as she told me about them. There were sad things too. Her oldest, Connie, had been in a difficult and dangerous relationship that had been tough for her to get away from. She was doing so much better now, and had been in a good and healthy relationship for years.

Then she told me about her youngest daughter, Dani, who was sixteen years old and seven months pregnant. Dawn said that when Dani had told her she was pregnant, she had suffered extreme *déjà vu*, thinking of when she had the same conversation with her parents. Dani was a different girl than Dawn. When Dawn talked to her about what the options were and what they should do, Dani told her mom defiantly, "Don't even talk to me about that. I'm having this baby and there's nothing you can do about it." That was the end of their conversation about options.

As she told me that, I was happy for Dani and how strong she was. But thinking about her made me wonder what happened with our own baby so many years before.

"Dawn, we never got to talk about what happened when you and I were in that same situation so long ago. Can we talk about it now?"

"I guess. What is there to talk about?"

"There are so many things that I never knew about. I got that phone call from Walt and Colleen telling me you were pregnant, then we met in your living room and I agreed not to see you for three years. We didn't talk again for thirty years after that. I never knew what happened after I left you. After awhile, I started to wonder if you had ever really been pregnant at all."

"I was."

"Oh."

The implication of those two words struck home and the sense of loss I had been holding at bay most of my life swept over me. The silence stretched out and sadness engulfed me. I was overwhelmed. My voice cracked when I tried to talk again.

"Dawn... I'm so sorry. I'm sorry for you and I'm sorry for me and I'm sorry for everything we lost. More than anything, I'm sorry for our baby. I'm sorry I wasn't smart or strong enough to figure a way to stop that from happening."

"I... I'm not sure what you mean."

"I mean I did everything I could to stop that from happening. When your mom and dad called me that night and told me you were pregnant, I told them I wanted to marry you so we could have the baby together. I told them that if they wouldn't let that happen, Terri would give me enough money to take care of the cost of having the baby and money to help raise it. Over and over, they kept telling me I had two choices: pay for the abortion or go to jail. I did everything I could, but I didn't do enough."

Now the silence stretched out on her end. After an eternity, she finally said "You're saying you wanted to keep the baby?"

"Yes, of course I did. Haven't you always known that?"

"No. That's not what Mom told me. She told me the abortion was your idea and you were glad to be rid of the baby and me. She told me you were living in Seattle, going out with college girls and happy to be away from me and the whole situation."

"Oh my God. Have you believed that all these years?"

"Yes."

"Oh, Dawn. No wonder you hated me all these years. You thought I got you pregnant, paid for the abortion, and happily disappeared forever."

"Yes."

It was the ultimate moment of clarity. Everything fell into place.

"Dawn, I don't know how to say this, except that your mom lied to you. When we lost our baby and I lost you, I lost everything. From then until right now, there's been a hole in my life that nothing could fill. Shit. Shit. Shit!"

I felt my face grow hot with anger. Colleen had been dead for twenty-five years, but whatever peace I had made with her in my mind evaporated.

"Shawn." Dawn's voice was sharp.

"What?" I heard anger and sharpness in my own voice too.

"I think we need to sit down together and talk."

My Angel Baby

Dawn was right. If we were ever going to really know each other again, we needed to sit down and talk. I had driven myself insane for years trying to make that happen, but with the opportunity at hand, I was nervous.

Before I sat down and talked to Dawn, I needed to finally do the right thing and talk to Adinah. As soon as the thought crossed my mind, my cell rang. I saw it was Adinah calling from Arkansas. I took that as a sign that the universe was encouraging me to be a grownup. I answered on the first ring.

"Hello."

"Hey, how are you doing?"

"I'm okay. The truth is I'm finally ready to talk to you about something I've been putting off for way too long."

"What's that?"

"Adinah, I want a divorce."

"You are such a bastard. You are *such* a bastard."

There's an immediate difference between men and women. When I get mad, I just get quiet. When Adinah got truly pissed off, she could instantly recall every wrong thing I had ever done with perfect clarity and recall. I spent the next forty minutes listening to a recitation of my sins. I listened attentively and didn't disagree.

In some obvious ways, I had been a good husband. I earned a good living, never had affairs and came home every night right after work. But in the ways that counted I failed every test. I was emotionally absent, unavailable, and unloving. I would have thought she would have been glad to be rid of me, and maybe she was. But she wanted to at least get a few parting shots first.

Eventually she grew quiet, and I was able to tell her what I was feeling.

"I really am sorry that I've hurt you. I tried not to hurt you for the last eight years and that only hurt you more. I won't do it anymore."

"So, this is really it then?"

"Yes."

She hung up.

A weight lifted off me. I did not enjoy that conversation in any way, but it was evidence of how little emotional investment I had left in the relationship. All I felt was relief that it was finally resolved. I felt bad that I had waited until Adinah was 2400 miles away before I had this talk with her. I suppose it was because of my lifelong fear of confrontation, a residue of the violence I experienced as a child. I associated confrontation with physical fights. Unfortunately, that unnamed fear caused me to put this off much longer than necessary.

I spent the rest of the day hanging out with my daughter, Samy, and my grandbaby, Amelia, who we called Millie. Millie was born on Samy's birthday the year before and was ten months old now. She was learning to walk and spent the day amusing us by doing her drunken sailor walk—one step forward, two steps back. Spending the day with Samy and Millie was just what I needed.

Dawn had to work for the next few days, but we still hadn't decided how we were going to meet. After a few days of negotiating, we finally settled on that Friday night. Dawn had to work, but she would be done by 5 PM. She worked in Tumwater, about an hour away from Enumclaw. I decided to drive us into Seattle. That would give us a chance to talk before we got to the restaurant. Even if dinner didn't go well, I would have the drive back to Tumwater to say goodbye.

When Friday finally arrived, I was so nervous I

couldn't work. I was afraid she wouldn't recognize me again, or would be shocked at how fat I was. I had gained 100 pounds since high school. Worst of all, I was afraid she just wouldn't care about me one way or the other. I left work earlier than necessary, because I couldn't take sitting behind my desk anymore. I stopped at Target and bought a new shirt and some deodorant, in case what I had put on that morning failed.

I ran into terrible traffic, but still got there in plenty of time. I got off I-5 at Exit 99 and drove straight to ACS, where Dawn worked. It was a tin, rundown building that wore years of neglect. I pulled into a spot off to the side, thinking that would give me a chance to see her approach. I wasn't sure I would recognize her, since I hadn't seen her in two and a half years.

I texted her to let her know where I was parked, then tried to stay cool. I made two CDs for filled with our songs from the '70s. I slid one into the CD player and *My Angel Baby* by Toby Beau started to play. I fidgeted in the driver's seat for a few minutes before I got out and leaned against the front fender, hoping in vain that it made me look a little cooler.

I watched people straggle out of the building. After a few minutes a woman walked toward me. I knew it wasn't Dawn because she was too young. She kept walking toward me until I had to smile at her. She smiled tightly back at me and I realized with a shock that it was her. She looked so young I didn't recognize her.

She was still the most beautiful woman I'd ever seen. She was shorter than I remembered–even though she stood on the curb and I stood on the ground, I was still taller–and her hair was longer and blonder than when I saw her last. She wore a long purple and grey top, black capris, and clunky sunglasses that hid her eyes.

My first thought was that it wasn't fair that she was still so good-looking after all these years. I had changed so much and she looked the same. I couldn't stop myself from staring.

"What?" she asked. I looked away from her and looked back. She had caught me staring. She was never bashful about calling me out. I shook my head and smiled nervously at her.

"Nothing. I'm just looking at you. You look so good." We paused awkwardly and smiled. I scrambled for something to say. "I thought I'd drive us into Seattle for dinner so we'd have a chance to talk on the way."

"That's fine. Let's go."

I wanted to walk around and open the car door for her, but she seemed guarded and distant. I climbed in the driver's side, waited for her to get in, and pulled back on to I-5 North. Dawn looked straight ahead or down at her phone. She was texting with her left hand. I'd forgotten she was left-handed.

I made casual conversation with her in between texts. We'd started to establish some intimacy in our emails and phone calls, but that seemed to have vanished. I felt like I was driving with a hitchhiker, vapidly trying to start a conversation. I could feel who she was so strongly, but I was a complete stranger to her. I turned the music up and told her I had made the CD for our drive. *I Will Still Love You* by Stonebolt was playing.

"Remember. This is the song you asked me to remember when I left back in 1979." She nodded absently and looked straight ahead, but didn't say anything. I began to think this was going to be a long night.

I finally broke the awkward silence that had been building. "So, I guess there are a few things I need to tell you about, now that we're face to face."

"Like what?"

"Pretty much the last thing I want to talk to you about is my marriage. But I need to. Adinah and I got married eight years ago. I knew it was a mistake immediately. I've been trying to end the marriage for years now, but I haven't been able to get it done."

"Have you ever tried saying 'I want a divorce?'"

"I hadn't until just a few days ago. I finally told her last Saturday. It's hard to explain why it took me so long. I feel guilty for marrying her in the first place and I guess I haven't wanted to admit I screwed up that bad."

"So if you're still married, what are you doing out with me? I'm not going to be any part of ending your marriage."

This wasn't going the way I had practiced it in my head. Things rarely did when I talked to Dawn.

"Believe me, everything to do with ending my marriage started long before we started talking again. I told her I didn't love her years ago, but that didn't seem to matter. We went to marriage counseling for years, but nothing happened because I was just trying to figure out the easiest way to end the marriage."

I took my eyes off the road for a second and turned my head to look at her, hoping for a clue about how she was taking this conversation, but she was hidden behind her dark glasses.

"Dawn, I know we don't really know each other anymore."

"That's right. You don't know me now. I'm not that little fifteen-year-old girl you left behind."

"Thank God. I loved that girl, but I've grown and changed over the years. Listen, I don't have any expectations about where we are right now. You don't owe me anything. If you want to have dinner with me and say goodbye forever, that's all right."

She didn't answer, but looked straight ahead, her jaw set.

I drove us through Capitol Hill traffic and pulled into the parking lot next to Charlie's on Broadway. Charlie's wasn't the fanciest place in Seattle, but it was one of my favorites. Terri and I used to go there for brunch on

Sundays, sitting by a front window watching the colorful locals wander by. The *maître d'* sat us in a quiet booth on the side of the restaurant. It was perfect for conversation.

We sat down opposite each other, and for the first time I got to look at her without sunglasses covering her eyes. She looked so much like her eighteen-year-old self, I would have known her anywhere. There was wariness in her eyes, but I also saw a flicker of warmth.

I kept looking for anything to break the ice, but nothing seemed to work. I tried to lighten the conversation.

"Did I mention that I like to cook now? I know I was completely helpless in the kitchen when you knew me before, but not anymore."

"Did you used to cook for the girls you went out with?"

I smiled and said, "Yeah, of course I did."

"And that worked for you, huh?"

It was clear I wasn't reaching her on any level. Finally, I realized there was no room for small talk.

"The other day in one of our emails," I said. "You mentioned that you resented me for a long time because I manipulated you into having sex when we were young."

"Yes, I did."

"Well, I want to talk to you about that, because I have a different memory than that."

"What do you mean?" Her eyes narrowed.

"I'm saying I have a different memory of that time. I remember that we had both decided that we weren't going to sleep together."

"Right."

"But that one time we were together on New Year's Eve, it happened because of you, not me."

"I'm not following you."

"On that day, you called me and started the conversation by asking me if I was still a virgin, remember?

Then you told me the address of the house where you were babysitting and told me to be there at ten. That was the reason we slept together."

She looked away. I could tell she was sifting through memories. Finally, I saw it click

"Oh my God." She paused and I waited for her to speak. She stared at the table, then looked up to meet my eyes. "You're right. Why didn't I remember that? Why did I remember things so differently?"

A sense of relief washed over me. I had been beginning to doubt my memory. I didn't know what I would do if she remembered things differently.

"Well, you were young. We never really talked after that night. I'm sure you built up some defenses and Walt and Colleen helped fill in the blanks the way they wanted you to remember things."

We had been at Charlie's for more than an hour, but it felt like we were just starting to break the ice. Our meals sat untouched in front of us. Our waiter came by to see if there was a problem and disappeared when we shook our heads.

Dawn began to poke at her food. We ate quietly and I could tell she was thinking about something. I was staring into my food when I heard her fork clink on her plate. I looked up to see her staring at me and shaking her head. She looked like she'd seen a ghost.

"Dawn, what?"

"You're my Shawn."

She said it like it was a new revelation.

I reached out and took her hand. It fit mine like always. I watched her firm veneer melt away and a tear streamed down her cheek.

"You were my Shawn."

"I always have been." Tears were in my eyes too.

"I'd lost who you were. But now I remember. I blocked out so much. Shawn, I'm sorry."

We sat quietly as the minutes stretched out. All conversation was lost in the moment of rediscovery. When I looked at the time, I saw that we had been sitting in a prime booth at Charlie's for three hours on a Friday night. No wonder the waiter kept wandering by every few minutes. I paid the bill and we headed out.

The ride back to Tumwater was much better than the drive up. We talked about Jerry and Chip and how we made fools of ourselves in KISS II. We talked about the music on the CDs and what each song made us remember.

I finally pulled back into the ACS parking lot and pulled alongside Dawn's red Grand Am. It was close to midnight and I knew Dawn needed to get back home to Dani. I put the car in park but didn't turn the engine off. I turned to Dawn and gave her every opportunity to let me down easy. It was a great night, but I knew there was still a chance she wouldn't want to see me again.

I wanted to give her an easy chance to walk away from me, so I said "Thank you for tonight. Getting to see and talk to you means so much to me. At the same time, I know you've got a lot going in your life. Dani's going to be having her baby soon, and you've got to find a new place to live. You've got your job. You've got a lot on your plate, and I don't know if you want to make room in your life for me right now."

Her eyes crinkled with laughter like they so often did when I said something dumb. "Yeah, everything's worked out great for me without you, hasn't it?"

I laughed my nervous laugh.

"Shawn. Turn off the car."

I turned off the car. When I turned in my seat, Dawn had turned as well, and was tantalizingly close to me. I saw the burning intensity I remembered so well. My heart raced, and I wondered if Dawn might be able to hear my heart beating in the sudden silence.

"Dawn, I know there are a lot of things we have to

figure out, and a lot of things to talk about, but I still feel so much for you. It's never changed."

"I know. I feel it too. But everything's moving so fast. We need to take it slow. Everything will work out the way it's supposed to. But for now, everything has to wait."

I got out of the car, walked around to the other side, and opened Dawn's door. I held her hand as we walked the few feet to her Grand Am. Everything felt so natural; the intervening years dissipated with each step. As so often happened with Dawn, I was swept up in the moment. I put my hand on her waist and pulled her toward me, kissing her gently.

"Dawn, I love you." I cringed as soon as I said it. I didn't want to meet Dawn's eyes, afraid of what I might see there. I saw only kindness and understanding when I did. She smiled at me gently.

"Taking it slowly, remember?"

I nodded and kissed her once more. An incredible sense of *déjà vu* swept over me as I was instantly transported back thirty years.

"You feel exactly the same," I said. I saw the shadow of her old smile play quickly across her lips. I looked away and sighed. I opened her door, she started the engine and left the parking lot. I stood motionless, staring after her until she was well out of sight.

I drove home filled with silent awe. I had dreamed about knowing Dawn again for so long that it felt unreal to me that I had just been with her. I couldn't believe how easy it was to talk and laugh with her. I had even held her in my arms ever so briefly. I hadn't slept much the night before because I was worried about our date, but adrenaline was coursing through me and I felt so high I wondered if I would ever come down.

As I had so often over the previous month, I needed to talk with my sister. She'd been dead for seven months, but I talked to her anyway.

"Terri Lee," I said. "Wherever you are, I hope you can hear me. You had to put up with me moping over my lost love for so many years. You deserve to see how everything is turning out. I messed up and told her I loved her on our first date, but it's gonna be okay. She already knew that. I have no idea what's coming next or how this is going to turn out, but I feel better than I can ever remember feeling in my life."

I talked to Terri all the way home.

And I Love You So

We didn't see each other the rest of that weekend, but we got together for a dinner date on Monday night. This time we stayed in Tumwater and ate at El Sarape. I should say we ordered food at El Sarape. We had so much to talk about that our food again went mostly uneaten.

There were so many memories and so much loss between us that we couldn't absorb it all at once. We talked in depth about what happened when we separated and where our lives went in the immediate aftermath. We always talked about our baby. We would never be able to heal that loss, but having each other to grieve with made it easier to bear. As incongruous as it sounds, we could have a tearful conversation one moment and be laughing together a few moments later. To an outsider, we probably looked like crazy people. Maybe we were.

After dinner we walked out into the warm summer air holding hands. I felt what it was that Dawn brought to my life; a connection so organic and unforced that it could never be duplicated. I trusted her so much that I was willing to let her see me with no pretense. The more I showed her, the more I felt she accepted me and loved me.

I walked her to my car, but before I opened the door for her, I pulled her to me and kissed her gently. I looked into her eyes and was overcome by how much I felt for her. We were taking it slow, but I had to speak.

"You're everywhere in me. You fill up my senses."

"Really, Shawn? John Denver? What's next? Barry Manilow?" Her deep brown eyes laughed at me as she called me out. This is the issue with loving someone who has the same frame of reference that you do. You can't slip anything by them.

I drove the few blocks back to where Dawn had parked her car. I was committed to keeping things light and breezy after all the heaviness of our dinner conversation. I purposefully steered clear of anything important when Dawn reached out her hand and laid it on my arm to get my attention.

"Shawn, I love you."

That got my attention. I looked at her. Without a thought, I said "I will never leave you, unless you send me away."

"Why would I ever do that? I love you Shawn, and I want you with me."

"I love you too, Dawn Adele, so much. We've both had so many losses in our lives that it's important that you know this. Now that I know you still love me, I'll never leave you."

I wanted to jump out of the car, climb up on the roof and shout as loud as I could. Instead, I closed my eyes, rested my head against hers, and cried softly. I felt peace settle over my soul like I had never known.

"You are such a girl," she said.

"And you're such a romantic," I said, laughing.

That was the end of taking it slow. Dawn managed to hold out for all of three days before she told me she loved me too. The first time she told me she loved me, we were laying on my Mom's floral couch in the little trailer in Mossyrock. Then, I had felt exulted and shocked. This time I sensed the pieces of my life falling into place. Thirty years had passed, and my life had always been a jangling medley of unmatched pieces. For once, everything fit together.

My first instinct was to ask Dawn to move in with me at my big house in Enumclaw. But we both knew that would be too much too soon. Dawn told me that she had never had a place that was her own. She had gone directly from Walt and Colleen's house to her marriage with Rick.

We spent a few weeks looking all over Centralia and Chehalis for a good place for her and Dani to live. We eventually found a duplex for them just a mile from Dawn's old house. That meant that if Dani wanted to go back to school and graduate after she had her baby, she'd be in the same school district. By the end of July, Dawn was settled into her new place. We went about finding out what our lives would be like together.

The short answer is that life was wonderful. We still had our challenges. Money was beyond tight, and we often felt like we were being pulled in ten different directions. But every day we spent together brought peace and happiness. It felt like a never-ending slumber party. Our nights—whether spent together or talking on the phone— were filled with laughter, teasing, and a connection that constantly grew stronger.

On August 18th, Dani had her baby boy, Yael. I always knew Dawn had a soft spot for babies, but Yael had her wrapped around his tiny finger from his first moment on this planet. He was a healthy, beautiful boy, and he brought so many gifts to the family. Dani had been a wild child before her pregnancy. She seemed to be heading down a difficult path. But everything changed once Yael arrived. It was amazing to witness Dani's transformation, and it was hard to believe that someone so small could have an impact so big on so many lives.

For the rest of August, I would have driven to Tumwater or Chehalis every day just to see Dawn for a few minutes, but we both knew that wasn't practical. We were so much like the teenagers we once were together. We just did not want to be apart.

One Sunday I spent the afternoon bothering Dawn, trying to convince her to let me come down the next day and buy her dinner. She wasn't sure she could get out of work early. Eventually, she emailed me.

> *Okay. I have to work tomorrow, but I really miss you too. I can get away for two or three hours after work, but let's skip dinner. You can figure out what I'm talking about. It's time to make up for lost time.*
> *Dawn*

My heart stopped. Since we had gotten back together, we had shared lingering goodnight kisses and necked in my car like teenagers. Now she was promising much more. I couldn't avoid the parallel between this email and the phone call I got from Dawn on New Year's Eve of 1978.

Everything had felt wrong that day. I was swept up in events beyond my control. This time, I knew we had waited long enough. I emailed her back.

> *I'll be there when you get off tomorrow. I'll be easy to spot—I'll be the one with the smile that will have to be surgically removed. Why does tomorrow seem so far away?*
> *Shawn*

That night, we weren't the same two innocent kids we were the first time around. But in some ways we were. Being with her that night washed away three decades of pain and uncertainty. I knew they would never return.

One thing had not changed. Time was still slippery when we were together. Our three hours were over before they started, and I had to drop Dawn back off at work.

Three days later, I flew back to Arkansas to pick up my fourteen-year-old daughter Sabrina. She had gone to Arkansas with Adinah and needed a ride home. My plan was to fly into Little Rock, meet Adinah to get the car, and drive back to Washington. A 2400-mile drive might seem a little daunting, but I had made it more than two dozen times over the years.

Sabrina didn't know I was in contact with Dawn when she left for her summer visit. I knew she would be thrilled. She and I had spent hundreds of hours together in the car, and we often amused ourselves by telling stories. Time and again, Sabrina would say, "Tell me another story about Dawn, Daddy." I think she liked seeing the different side of me that came out when I talked about Dawn. Those stories I told Sabrina as we zipped along the interstate toward Arkansas were the origin of this book.

While she was in Arkansas, I had told her I was in contact with Dawn again. She was surprised and thrilled when I told her that Dawn and I were together. Having Dawn enter our lives was something like having a character from a book step off the page. I think Sabrina had partly believed the stories I told her were a fairy tale.

Sabrina was another perfect fit in our lives. Everything finally felt right. My house was big, but we were doing a good job of filling it up with me, Sabrina, Samy, and Millie.

On the first Saturday of September, Dawn and I decided to drive to Mossyrock. It had been years since either of us had been there, and we thought it would be fun to revisit the place where our story started. I made another mix CD to listen to while we drove with songs like *Rush Hour* by Jane Wiedlin, *What's Up* by Four Non-Blondes, and *Kryptonite* by 3 Doors Down. Just for fun, I led off the CD with the song Adam Sandler sang to woo Drew Barrymore in *The Wedding Singer*: *Grow Old With You*.

We rolled into Mossyrock holding hands just like when we were returning from our dates all those years ago. This time it was our kids who set our curfew. We drove through town, which took all of thirty seconds. Then we went for a ride on the back roads we used to travel every day before school. It was like stepping into a time machine and coming out again in 1978.

That feeling lasted until we drove down Damron Road and found our old houses. My old 1965 double-wide trailer was still there, although whoever owned it didn't keep up the outside like my step-dad always had. When he lived there, every sidewalk was swept, the lawn was mowed like a golf course, and no weed dared to grow in his garden. Now everything looked much smaller and shabbier. I almost didn't recognize it. Dawn's house was almost unrecognizable too. It was remodeled and built out, so that Dawn's old window was gone. It looked nicer, but also very different. I pulled into my old driveway and we sat for a moment. We had shared so much history on that spot that I wanted to mark it in my memory one last time.

We had to make one more stop before leaving. Just before Highway 12, I turned right and climbed the gravel road to Doss Cemetery. We cruised past the spot where I asked Dawn to marry me in November of 1978. There had been trees for me to hide behind then. Now the land was cleared and a real estate office had popped up.

Everything was exactly the same once we passed the office. We made it to the top of the hill and curved to the right. The cemetery stretched out before us. This was our sacred ground—the site of the best moments of our lives. I coasted to the bottom of the cemetery and parked in our spot.

I looked at Dawn.

"Can you believe we used to have the nerve to come here and get naked together?"

"We were young."

"Yeah."

"Adventurous."

"Yeah."

"Horny."

I laughed, lifted my eyebrows, and shot her a look.

"Not on your life, Patrick Shawn Inmon. I am not a teenager anymore. I'm not that flexible either."

I sighed with mocking exaggeration. I was kind of glad she shut me down because I don't think my back would have withstood that. I smiled and felt wondrously happy to be sitting in this spot with my girl. In all our years apart, I never let myself dream of a day this good.

The CD player started to play Warren Zevon's career coda, *Keep Me In Your Heart,* and the funniest thing happened. Raindrops began to gather on our windshield and I felt the moment overwhelming me. I hopped out of the car and scrambled over to Dawn's side. Unlike the first time I did this, I didn't let a little mud stop me from doing it right. I got down on one knee in the grass. Dawn was smiling easily, confident that I was joking around.

But I wasn't joking. I was less prepared than the first time I asked her to marry me. I didn't even have a ring. I was broke and my career was in the toilet. I was a worse marriage prospect than I was back in '78. But I didn't care. I did have one thing: the certainty that Dawn was the one I was supposed to be with forever.

I took her hand and looked deeply into her eyes.

"Dawn Adele, I have always loved you. I will always love you. Will you marry me?"

Her smile faltered as her eyes grew wide. She finally understood I was completely serious. She seemed to consider her options for about a second and a half. It felt like a lifetime. She reached out and ran her fingertips across my cheek.

"Yes, Shawn. I will marry you." It was the second time I heard her say those words.

It began to rain harder. As I leaned in to kiss her, rainwater ran off the roof of the car and down my neck. It felt wonderful. I met her eyes and smiled a smile that started at my toes. Another weight–another lifetime uncertainty–was lifted away. I felt as happy as a kid on the last day of school. A lifetime of possibilities opened in front of me.

"Shawn."

"Yes, baby?"

"You're getting wet."

"Don't care."

At that moment, I didn't care about that or anything else in the world. In ninety days I had gone from an inch-by-inch death to feeling more optimistic and content than ever.

There was another parallel between the first time I asked Dawn to marry me and this time around. We still had a few hurdles to jump, just as we had in 1978. Adinah and I had agreed on how everything would proceed with our divorce. I agreed to pay the cost of the proceedings, but I didn't have the money yet. Also, Dawn hadn't so much as spoken to Rick in five years, and I knew that the prospect of negotiating the end of their marriage filled her with anxiety. What's more, I was sure we would have to pay for that too.

There was also the question of the wedding. We had three options: elope; have a small backyard family wedding, or throw a full bash with 150 of our closest friends. We immediately scratched off the eloping. We couldn't conceive of making this commitment without our daughters there.

Ultimately, we decided to have the full wedding on a budget. The only downside was that we had no idea how we would pay for it. Dawn wanted an autumn wedding, so to give us a little more time to get our divorces settled and raise some money, we set our date for October, 2010. It was more than a year in advance.

Breathe (In the Air)

In late September 2009, I looked at the calendar and saw an opportunity. October 16th would be exactly one year before our wedding day, and it fell on a Friday. I dubbed this our *pre-versary* and scheduled a celebration. I got a great rate on a room at Hyatt Place in downtown Seattle.

I had lived in Seattle from 1978 through 1985, and spent much of that time wandering through the city, thinking of Dawn. I wanted to erase those sad memories once and for all. I had a feeling that Dawn had never seen the city through my eyes.

Early on the morning of the 16th, I texted Dawn in Chehalis and told her to hurry up so we could start our adventure.

It was afternoon by the time we got to Seattle, and we were able to check into our room at Hyatt Place. We walked into the elegant lobby feeling like teenagers who had ditched our chaperones. Our room was on the 20th floor and had a view of the Seattle skyline.

While Dawn was in the bathroom getting unpacked, I opened my suitcase and took out the dozen roses I had bought that morning.

I quickly arranged the roses, and hustled around the room laying out votive candles in little candle holders. I unpacked my iPod and started the playlist I made just for the trip. This was romance on a budget. When Dawn emerged from the bathroom, she was surprised by my preparations and agreed that my pre-versary idea was alright after all.

I was thrilled to find that Laserium was still around, just as it was when we tried to go in '78. That meant I could finally fulfill my promise to take Dawn. We left the Hyatt and walked across the street to Westlake Center to catch the monorail to the Seattle Center. On our way to the monorail station, we wandered into a funky little clothing store where I saw a patchwork hoody jacket emblazoned with peace signs. Dawn's fashion sense leaned toward '70s casual, so I asked her to try it on. The sleeves dangled past her fingers. It was adorable on her, so I bought it for her while she continued to browse.

We boarded the monorail, which was built for the 1962 World's Fair, just like Seattle Center. Two minutes later, we got off at the base of the Space Needle and walked to the Pacific Science Center. I purchased two tickets to see *Laser Floyd* and saw that we were first in line. We would get our choice of places on the floor to lay and watch the show. When I was young, I thought that only old people sat in the seats. Now that I was one of those old people, there was no way I wasn't going to lie flat on my back.

The planetarium had aged pretty well. The carpet was a little worn, but it looked almost exactly like I remembered it from thirty years before. The lights dimmed just after we lay down, and Pink Floyd's *Dark Side of the Moon* began. Dawn rested her head on my chest.

I've heard *Dark Side of the Moon* from start to finish hundreds of times. I know every word, every musical flourish, and every odd sound effect. I believed I had sucked all the musical marrow from that bone. But lying there with Dawn next to me, I was overcome with emotion. When Clare Torry unleashed her otherworldly banshee wail on *The Great Gig in the Sky,* I felt lifted up out of my body toward the laser images on the ceiling. I have never done drugs, but I managed my own little trip that night. I was drained when the show was over. I also felt like we had somehow connected another circle we left open thirty years ago.

I finally had a nice little spurt of real estate activity in the first quarter of 2010. These bursts were few and far between. I knew this might be the only one I would get before our wedding, so I had to make every dollar count.

The first thing I did was begin looking for a ring. I began haunting Craigslist in search of the perfect ring. After several weeks of checking every few hours, I found what I thought was the perfect ring. I showed Dawn the listing to see what she thought. As soon as I saw the expression on her face, I knew it was the ring for us. It was going to be hard to surprise her with the ring after showing it to her, but I did my best. I told her the ring had already been sold. That was true, it had been sold–to me.

With the wedding rings finally in hand, I set about planning a surprise for Dawn Adele. I asked her to get Valentine's Day weekend off. Since our forced separation had happened on Valentine's Day weekend, I told her I wanted to celebrate our first one back together in style. In truth, I had more than that planned. Ever since my impromptu proposal at Doss Cemetery in September I had wanted to ask her again in a more formal setting. My budget was a concern, but thanks to Priceline and Groupon, I was able to put everything together.

Once again, I got a great price on a beautiful room. This time it was the Grand Hyatt in downtown Seattle. I knew that the Grand Hyatt was right next to one of my favorite restaurants, Ruth's Chris Steak House. The final piece fell into place when I got a Groupon for a half-price helicopter tour of Seattle.

We got to the Grand Hyatt early on the afternoon of February 13th. When I told the very sweet girl at the check-in counter what I was planning to do that night, she tapped a few keys.

"In that case, I would like to do something special for you. Let me see what I've got available." Moments later she said smiled at me, handed me a key card and said, "I think you'll be very happy with this room."

She was right. For the price of a rock-bottom Internet bid, she upgraded us to a full suite, with a kitchen, dining room, huge master bedroom, and a gorgeous marble bathroom. Who says romance is dead? I hadn't told Dawn we were getting a suite like this, because I didn't know. When I opened the door to our suite, Dawn's eyebrows shot up.

"Is this really our room?"

I acted as if this had been the plan all along, and we took a tour of what would be our home for the next 24 hours. There were huge windows looking out on the Seattle skyline and the Space Needle. Everything in the suite was incredible. There were elegant furnishings, a flat-screen TV, and a beautiful kitchenette with granite countertops. It was bigger than my first two apartments put together. We didn't have too much time to enjoy it, because I had scheduled a helicopter ride over the city.

We drove through downtown and along Boeing Field to the Seattle Helitours building. Dawn questioned me more and more as we cut through the industrial section of town. I wouldn't answer her, which drove her crazy.

We got to Seattle Helitours and I finally broke down and told her my plan. I was a little nervous about whether she would want to go, since she's afraid of heights. But she smiled and said she couldn't wait.

Seattle Helitours used classic helicopters. Ours was old, but it was cool looking. The pilot was a great tour guide. We flew over Lake Washington, the Ballard Locks, and circled the Space Needle. We even buzzed Bill Gates' house. I'm sure he loved being part of the itinerary. I had brought our rings in case I was again overcome with impatience and asked her to marry me again while we were up in the air. As anxious as I was, I managed to keep the rings in my pocket for the whole flight.

We returned to the hotel after our tour. I changed into my suit and Dawn put on a new dress. We cleaned up pretty well. Dawn glowed with the same inner light and beauty that she always did. I felt privileged to be her escort, as I did on our Prom night.

I had called ahead and spoken to the *maître d'* at Ruth's Chris, so everything was ready for us when we got there. It was 8 PM on the Saturday night of Valentine's Day weekend, so the lobby was packed with people waiting to be seated. We were having a blessed day, and we would have been happy to wait all night.

I felt nervous again once we were seated. I've come to accept that this is an unavoidable side effect of being around a girl I care about so much. I calmed myself down enough to enjoy our surroundings and the fabulous food we ordered. We both ordered a rare petit filet mignon, and shared a Caesar salad. After dinner, we ordered a dessert to split, since calories don't count on special occasions. Once our table was cleared, Dawn glowed with happiness. I saw my opportunity.

I stood up and moved around to the side of the table. Dawn asked me where I was going, but I just shook my head. I couldn't speak. I got down on one knee, completely blocking the aisle. All around us, I heard conversations stop and the whispers begin. I ignored them and focused on the only person in the world who mattered.

Dawn's eyes were large and she looked uneasy about suddenly being the center of attention. I took her hand in mine and slipped the rings out of my pocket. "Dawn Adele, for the third and final time in our life, I want to ask. Will you marry me?"

There were tears in her eyes, and her answer was barely audible.

"Yes." She smiled and my heart beat a little faster, just

like it always did when she looked at me like that.

I slipped the rings on her finger and she gasped a little when she saw they were the rings we had looked at together. "You said these were sold!"

"They were. To me."

Behind me, I heard four men who were on their own Valentine's Day dates.

"Well, what'd she say?" They asked.

I smiled and gave a thumbs-up. They stood and applauded. Much of the section around us joined in. I finally stood, acknowledging the nods and good wishes. I wiped my brow and sat back down.

It had been spontaneous and natural when I knelt in the rain in Doss Cemetery and asked Dawn to marry me. This time it was relaxed and easy with the outcome no longer in doubt. We were two small-town kids, playing dress-up and having our moment in the big city. I held Dawn's hand across the table and admired the way the candlelight sparkled in her new diamond. Our eyes locked and I smiled. I was ecstatic to know that our lives would be intertwined as long as we were both alive.

God of Thunder

Now that we were together almost all the time, I had time to ask Dawn questions that troubled me over the years. One of the things I wondered about was why she had propositioned me on New Year's Eve, 1978. It was so out of character that I was never able to understand why it had happened.

When I asked Dawn about it, she said she thought I was at the UW, going out with college girls, and slowly losing interest in the young girl I left behind. She thought having sex was the best way to hold on to me. She was wrong, but at least it helped me understand why she had acted that way.

I had also wondered what she had thought about KISS II. Did she think it was cool at all, or was it just an embarrassing memory?

"I loved you in spite of KISS II," she said, laughing. "Not because of it."

Of course, it didn't matter. KISS II died when we blew our sound system in the spring of 1978. I had worn the costume when I dressed up a few times for Halloween but I left even that behind by the early '80s. Sabrina often asked me to "do Gene Simmons, Daddy," but I always declined. That was all behind me.

Then I joined Facebook in August 2009. I found a lot of old friends waiting there for me. Joining Facebook was a big step for me. I had avoided social media because I was unhappy with my life and didn't want to be in contact with anyone. I was frozen and isolated, and thought I would always stay that way. Then Dawn and I happened, and everything changed. Those first few months after I joined, it felt like a high school reunion. I reconnected with dozens of old friends I hadn't spoken to in many years.

One of those old friends was Tracey Antrobus. I sent her a friend request and got a message back immediately.

> *Hi Shawn! You will NOT believe this. I was driving home on Monday night and was thinking about the All-Class Reunion next year and about you and Jerry and how awesome it would be to have KISS II, play a "reunion concert"! On my way back to Vancouver I saw your Facebook request come through on my Blackberry. I just sat there and laughed. I haven't talked to you in 30 years, only to have me thinking about you the same time you were thinking about me. Maybe you need to think about a KISS II revival! It's awesome to see you and Dawn together. Take good care and give Dawn a hug for me.*
>
> *Tracey*

I sent a message back to Tracey thanking her for the laugh. No one would want to see me onstage wearing spandex. It wasn't going to happen.

Over the next few months, someone would occasionally drop me a Facebook message along the lines of "do you remember that crazy thing that you and Jerry did with KISS?" Suggestions of a KISS II reunion persisted until April 2010, when I got this message from my old friend and classmate Alice Guenther:

> *Hi. We are planning a multi-class party at the Mossyrock Community Center during the All-Class Reunion at the end of July. There will be dancing, songs from our era and we'll all have a great time. Anyway, we were wondering if KISS*

*II would like to secretly surprise everyone and
come out of retirement, or come ALIVE (as my
husband put it), and perform a couple songs for
good old times? I realize that the costumes and
face paint are probably gone, but we think it
would be fun! Think it over–talk to the rest of the
band. You know how much work it would require
better than the rest of us.*

Alice

I'm not sure why, but suddenly it didn't seem so
unreasonable to think about getting back together. A few
months earlier, Dawn, me, Jerry, and his wife, Lynn, got
together for the first time in many years. We started with
lunch, but it stretched into a five hour conversation about
everything. Ever since then, we'd been looking for a
reason to hang out together, and this seemed like a way to
make it happen.

I called Jerry and told him what Alice had asked us.
We decided to get together the next day and figure out if it
was possible. It was already mid-April, and the All-School
Reunion was just three months away.

The next afternoon, I met Jerry at the Starbucks on
Meridian in Puyallup. I brought my 18" tall Gene
Simmons statue for inspiration. Jerry sat down across
from me, and I pointed to the statue.

"What do you think? Can you make me look like
that?"

This was no idle question. Jerry's hobby was making
period-accurate armor. He took several minutes to look
over Gene's Destroyer-era costume, making calculations
and imagining things I couldn't even guess at.

"I can make this."

"Okay, then. The next question is whether or not we
want to do this? It's been a long, long time."

"I can tell you this," said Jerry. "We're not going to do

all that work just to show up and wave and do a couple of songs. I think we should do four shows and I think we could sell out the gym."

I was skeptical. Our roles hadn't changed after all these years. Jerry was the big idea man, and I was the wet blanket.

We decided to give it a try. I tried to contact Bill Wood, who was our Ace Frehley, and Chip Lutz, our old Peter Criss, while Jerry got to work on designing my costume. We had decided to stay with the same era of KISS as before. It was clear that my costume was going to be the most challenging to construct.

We hadn't performed in thirty years. We didn't know if the rest of the band had any interest in reuniting, and we didn't have any costumes. On top of that, I didn't know if anyone wanted to see fifty-something guys in spandex and platforms lip-syncing to thirty-year-old music. I also had my doubts about whether the Mossyrock School District and the All-School Reunion Committee would welcome us with open arms.

I put out a teaser about a possible KISS II reunion on Facebook. The reaction was overwhelmingly positive. Our roadie from the '70s, Jeff Hunter, said he would help us out. On Facebook, he said, "If we manage to pull this off, KISS II will have had a long career. Not a good career, but a long one." I thought that was a pretty good motto for KISS II. Jeff agreed to be our stage manager, which meant that he took care of pretty much everything.

I tried to contact Bill Wood through his wife's Facebook page. For a while, she said he might be interested. But in the end he decided he didn't want to play with us.

Chip Lutz was tough to track down. He wasn't on Facebook yet, but eventually we found a tax record in his name in Tacoma. Jerry and I drove up there, but Chip was at work. His father-in-law was home and promised to have him call us, which he did.

Most of the interested parties gathered at the Weibles' big house in Puyallup: Dawn and I, Chip and his wife, and of course, our hosts Jerry and Lynn Weible plus their kids. It took us about thirty seconds to start insulting each other like we were all still in high school. Chip looked great, and we even threw an impromptu practice together in the basement. The chemistry all felt right, but in the end, we couldn't talk Chip into joining, which left us an Ace and a Peter short of reviving KISS II.

It turned out that we were in luck. The answer to our missing Ace was right in front of us all along. Jerry's oldest daughter, Brittany, was a guitarist. She had been a KISS fan since she had been able to walk. We rehearsed with Brittany in the role of Ace. Jerry and I were worried because she was so good that we knew she was going to blow us off the stage.

In mid-May, the Weible-Inmon clan drove to Mossyrock to attend the planning session for the All-School Reunion. We planned to do several shows, charge ten bucks a head, and give all the proceeds to the All-School Reunion committee. We had no interest in trying to make any money off this event. It was about fun and nostalgia.

I've often thought that a committee is the place where good ideas go to die, and this was no exception. The committee was upset that we had waited so long before springing this idea on them. They also didn't want to allow people from outside of Mossyrock to attend any event held at the school. Truth be told, they weren't crazy about having KISS music played on school grounds for several hours at a stretch. At one point, one of the older citizens of Mossyrock said she didn't want the kind of riff-raff we would attract to town.

We walked out of the meeting feeling a little bemused. We were without a venue and more determined than ever to stage our concert. We immediately dubbed the shows *The Riff-Raff World Tour—Mossyrock*. The one positive aspect was that the people on the Committee had referred to Jerry and me as "kids" on more than one occasion.

We spent the whole ride home brainstorming ideas about how to get around this roadblock. Before we got home, we remembered that the old G Theater in town had gone out of business. Before that, they had built a pretty decent stage in front of the screen. As soon as the G was brought up, it was all we could think about. It was where I saw my first movie ever, *Mary Poppins*. It was where I saw Jenny Agutter go skinny-dipping in *Walkabout,* providing me with my first lesson in female anatomy. It was also where Dawn and I went to see movies when I didn't have enough gas to get us out town to the Fox Theater or the drive-in.

It took us several days, but I learned the names of the current theater owners—Mike and Vicky Howard. They had bought it some years before from Paul Ghosn, the "G" in the G Theater. I called Mike and Vicky, and they didn't sound all that crazy about the idea of opening their shuttered building for several nights so that we could pretend to play KISS music. But I've been a salesman all my life, and before I got off the phone, Mike agreed to at least meet with us to discuss it.

The next day, Jerry and I drove down to Mossyrock and met Mike at the theater. Neither of us had been in the theater for thirty years, so even though it was frayed around the edges and smelled musty, it was incredible being there. It was much larger in my memory. In fact, it was pretty small, holding about 120 people. It was an odd feeling to walk through the theater. The snack bar was smaller than a coat closet and the old-fashioned seats and mid-century architecture were amazing to see.

Sure enough, there was a great stage right in front of the screen. I knew it would be a perfect place to play. I knew at once that this was the perfect venue for KISS II, despite Mike having given no sign that he would relent.

We sat on the stage and talked to Mike for a long time. He asked about our background, what we did for a living, and wondered what we were going to do with the money we made. We told him we had formed a scholarship fund for Mossyrock High School students and named it after an MHS grad that had recently passed away–Michael Sean Deasy, Jr. During high school, Mike Deasy had worked in the G Theater as a projectionist. It all seemed perfect. We also told him that our core value was that we wanted to leave any place we ever played in better condition than when we found it.

Mike scanned the dust-covered seats and walls. "That shouldn't be too hard. You know, people come through here all the time, wanting to use the theater for one thing or another, but I have a feeling about you guys. You can use the theater for your shows."

"That's awesome, Mike. Now about our budget…" I began to tell him that our budget was approximately zero when he cut me off.

"I don't want any money. How about instead you give me tickets so I can take my family to see the show?"

Just like that, we had our venue.

Thanks to Jerry, our costumes were coming along nicely. We had our Ace and just needed a new Peter Criss. Our first plan was to use Jerry's son, Connor. He was an excellent drummer and would have been perfect for the part. Unfortunately, he said no.

Brittany and Jerry remembered their neighbor, Jeff Johnson. They saw him playing drums in his garage and noticed the classic KISS posters on the walls. That weekend, Jerry and I walked to Jeff's house and asked if he would be interested in playing the Catman in a lip-syncing KISS tribute band. That's probably not a request you get every day. Jeff took it in stride and told us he would consider it. We took that to mean he wanted to talk it over with his wife. A few days later, Jeff called us and told us he was in.

Against all odds, KISS II was back.

Over the next two months, we spent many days in Mossyrock, getting the G Theater ready for the show and spreading the word. A month before the performance, we held an all-day cleaning party/dress rehearsal. I talked a reporter from Centralia's *The Daily Chronicle* named Brandon Swanson into spending the day with us. He brought a video camera, a reporter's notebook and a keen sense of humor. This made him the perfect reporter to cover KISS II. Brandon's story about us ended up being more than we could have dreamed. The video story he created showed the whole history of the band. It ended up being the third most popular video the *Chronicle* produced that year, trailing only a story about *Making Babies in Glenoma* and *In Search of Sasquatch*. The print story was even better. On the day of our shows, *The Daily Chronicle* featured us like rock 'n roll gods, sprawled across the masthead on the front page of the paper. Inside, they devoted a two-page spread to the story they called "Mossy Rock City." It was a little overwhelming for a recently un-retired KISS air/tribute band.

The 30th of July was a day for the ages. That was the day of our first two shows. More importantly, it was also the day Dawn's divorce became final, and she had to be in court that morning. As if that wasn't enough, it was also her last day working at ACS. It was a job she had mostly loved for six years. It was an emotional day for everyone, but especially for Dawn.

Jerry arranged to have two full-sized RVs delivered to the parking lot outside The G Theater, so we had a place to crash and get our makeup and costumes on. When we showed up with our full entourage of twenty people, it was like the circus came to town. There had been some concern around Mossyrock about our shows, but most everyone got in the spirit of the occasion.

Someone filed a complaint with the Mossyrock Fire Chief, Matt Hadaller, about unsafe fire conditions in the theater. Matt inspected the site and stuck around to help us make a few corrections. On the day of the show, he put all of us on top of their shiniest fire truck and drove us around town and out to Riffe Lake, with sirens blaring to help promote our show.

We were a little concerned about the turnout for our first show, but there was no need to worry. The crowds were big and enthusiastic. Standing outside the concrete back entrance of the G Theater, waiting to go onstage for the first time in 32 years, I looked at Jerry in amazement.

"This is a life experience we'll never forget," Jerry said, standing in full seven-inch platform boots, spandex pants, and a star-covered vest open to the waist.

I smiled my best Gene Simmons demon smile and looked down at the nearly twenty pounds of leather I was wearing, ending in my own platforms that looked remarkably like demon heads.

I looked at Jerry and knew he was the best kind of family you can have in this life—the kind you choose.

"There's no one else I'd rather do this with, Weib. Now let's go pretend to be rock stars!"

And we did.

At Last

My only real problem since asking Dawn to marry me was figuring out how I was going to pay for our wedding. When I had my cluster of real estate closings at the beginning of 2010, I'd been afraid I might have to make it last a long time. That proved correct, as I had very few closings for the rest of the year. But my favorite quotation has always been "Jump, and a net will appear". I continued to jump, and the net always appeared. But there were times I was pretty close to the ground when it caught me.

Each time Dawn reminded me of something we needed for the wedding, she would ask, "Are you sure we can do this?"

"Yes, of course," I answered. Then I would add silently, *I think.*

Every time I felt overwhelmed, a friend or family member would pop up and say, "I want to do this for you." We were overwhelmed by the support we received. Even though my entire office of realtors was suffering like I was, they still got together and bought us our wedding cake. If not for their generosity, we might have settled for wedding Twinkies.

One of my agents, Lisa Williams, volunteered her twin sister Lori to provide flowers at cost. They turned out exactly like we hoped. She worked miracles for us on our miserly budget.

An old friend from Mossyrock, Sherry Blakely, told us that she often planned weddings and that she wanted to help make our day perfect for us. She supplied almost all the decorations we used. Most importantly, she prompted us to ask questions that hadn't yet crossed our minds.

Jerry drew five larger-than-life posters representing us at various stages through our lives, and we used them to decorate the hall. He had always been my favorite artist, and having his originals hanging at our wedding meant so much. Jerry's wife, Lynn, managed to be in the exact right place, helping in exactly the right way, all without attracting attention.

Jeff Hunter proved to be just as adept in the kitchen as he was organizing and managing KISS II. He took over the food preparation for our reception. With his help, we managed to feed 120 of our closest friends for just $300.

Dawn's friend Jessica showed up at our rehearsal dinner–which was really just pizza–and helped us organize everything, while her husband Josh set up his huge sound system in preparation to be our reception deejay.

Dawn chose her daughter Connie as her maid of honor. Her daughter Dani, my daughter Sabrina, and Dawn's best friend Sheilah were her bridesmaids. My groomsmen were Jerry, and Connie and Dani's boyfriends, Jamie and Daniel. My 'best man' was my daughter Samy. As my main confidante during the early stages of my reconnection with Dawn, she fully deserved that honor. Plus, she really looked rockin' in her tux.

Sheilah's husband Darren, officiated. It was appropriate. In her darkest days, Dawn often turned to Sheilah and Darren for comfort and assistance. They were always there for her, earning my eternal love and gratitude.

When Dawn and I were together in the '70s, it often felt like the world was conspiring to keep us apart. Now the opposite was true. It seemed that everyone we knew was working to make sure our day was special. Our karmic scales were finally balancing out.

I spent most of my wedding day in the kitchen helping Jeff and several other friends prepare dinner. This is the price you pay for a big wedding on a budget—you get to be the groom/prep cook. I thought I would be nervous, but a perfect calm settled over me. I had loved Dawn for 35 years. Making it official was nothing to be nervous about.

About two hours before the ceremony, I turned to Jeff.

"I think it's time for me to write my vows." He looked at me like I was kidding, but I wasn't. I always worked best under pressure, and I already had in mind what I wanted to say. I sat down and the words poured out of me. I wrote my vows in fifteen minutes. I still had plenty of time to chop Romaine for our Caesar salad before getting dressed.

Of course, I had spent months obsessing over the wedding music. Nick Cave's *Into My Arms* played while Brittany and Morrigan Weible lit our candles. I chose Don Mclean's version of *And I Love You So* for the bridal party entrance. It was a song I often listened to when we were apart, and it captured the spirit of appreciation for how love can change your life and your perspective. The bridesmaids entered to Alan Jackson's *Red Like a Rose*, which felt perfect and was Dawn's choice.

Dawn entered to Etta James's *At Last*. What else could it have been?

There had been much speculation among the wedding party as to when I would cry during the ceremony. But I had no tears as I heard those soaring strings and Etta's smoky voice. My spirit lifted up and out of me, and I felt like I might follow it to the rafters, like an untethered helium balloon.

Dawn had hoped that her brother Brian would be able to make it up from California to give her away. He wasn't able to make it, so Jerry filled in admirably.

When Dawn appeared on Jerry's arm, every eye was on her. She was radiant. She was as lovely a bride as there has ever been. My throat constricted but I held back the tears. I had waited a lifetime to see Dawn walk down the aisle to me and I didn't want my vision blurred.

Jerry smiled when they finally reached me. He had been one of the first people I confided in when I realized I was falling in love with Dawn all those years ago. It was sweet that he was the one to present her hand to me now.

We stood in front of so many people we loved, held hands, and reveled in the moment. I wanted to stop time to take inventory. My oldest daughter Desi hadn't been able to make the trip out from Kentucky, but we still had four daughters standing there with us. This was the moment they went from 'my girls' and 'your girls' to 'our girls.' Playing happily at our feet were Samy's daughter Millie and Dani's son Yael, our flower girl and ring bearer. They were oblivious to the solemnity of the moment, and were focused only on collecting the flower petals that were scattered around.

Something deep inside me had felt wrong for as long as I could remember. By measures both large and small, that wrongness had slowly dissolved over the previous eighteen months. Now I knew I could release it forever.

I've been told that I need to accept what's in my life, to understand that every grain of sand is exactly where it needs to be. I tilted against that windmill for so long that I wearied of the battle. Now I felt that idea come into sharp focus in my heart.

This time it was Dawn who had a surprise for me on our wedding day. I make speeches regularly in my life, but I don't know if Dawn had ever spoken in front of a large crowd. I needed my reading glasses and my notes to get through my vows, but Dawn stared at me squarely in the eyes and spoke from her heart, with no notes at all.

What a journey - just a few years ago, I never would have believed I could be standing here with you. If we hadn't been separated by fate, I believe we would still be together today, but I don't know if we would have this same appreciation and love for each other.

You are my best friend, my love, my soulmate. Between us, we have brought five of the most beautiful and strong women into the world–our daughters, our family. We have a love for each other that grows stronger every day.

I have two promises: I promise to thank God every morning for bringing you back to me, and I promise to appreciate everything you are and everything you do for me. Thank you for coming with me on this journey.

With tears running down my face, it was my turn to speak.

Dawn Adele, I love you more each day. That means I love you more at this moment than I ever have before, yet this is the least I will ever love you in our life together.

These are my vows: I vow to always get things down off the top shelf for you without making fun of you because you can't reach it. I vow to always open doors for you, even your car door when it's raining really hard. I vow to bring you your first cup of coffee every day for the rest of your life. Most important to you, I vow to always be your protector from spiders large and small.

At that moment, I paused and thought back to the summer evening when she had told me she loved me again. Still.

"Dawn Adele," I said. "Until I draw my last breath, I

will never leave you."

Darren said the words I had been waiting all my life to hear. "You may kiss your bride."

I did.

We exited the hall to Stevie Ray Vaughan's *The House is Rockin (Don't Bother Knockin')*. We were older, but we weren't dead. Plus, we thought it would embarrass our kids.

We stood outside the hall in the late afternoon sunshine and soaked in the love and good wishes from our friends. I was so happy to see my friends, Bob and Karen Lichtenwalter, who had driven all the way from Maine to attend our ceremony. We didn't have much in the way of family there, outside of our kids, but several of my relatives from my real dad's side of the family made the drive. It thrilled me to see them.

When we went back inside the hall, we had our first dance as a married couple. We had gone back and forth for months over what song we should dance to first. We had initially thought Heatwave's *Always and Forever* would be ideal, but eventually realized that it reminded us a little too much of some of the hard times we had gone through. A few months before the wedding we were driving down I-5 together when The Hollies' *The Air That I Breathe* came on the radio. We knew we didn't need to look any further.

As that unmistakable opening chord played, I proudly held Dawn's hand and we walked onto the deserted dance floor. I held her close and thought back to our other memorable dances together. I had first discovered I had feelings for her while dancing to *Stairway to Heaven* at my sixteenth birthday party. I knew I had fallen in love with her on the floor of Hollywood Hollywood. Of course, I would never forget dancing barefoot in the living room of the trailer on Prom night.

Every dance together was a step for us, and this was a

big one. I stared deeply into Dawn's hazel eyes and smiled with complete contentment.

When I was a young man, I thought the word *contentment* meant settling, giving up. It was only at that moment, watching Dawn as she moved gracefully around the room in her wedding gown, that I realized that contentment could be so good. It was peace. It was an absence of fear. It was the best feeling I had ever known.

By the end of the evening, the crowd dwindled to a few old friends we went to school with, our kids, and our KISS II family. They helped us load our presents and divide up the leftover food and wine. Then they swept and mopped the hall so we would get our deposit back.

Your friends will come to your wedding. Your family will be there to sweep up afterward.

When we were finally ready to go, we walked outside to see that the kids had decorated our car for the honeymoon. They had attached some sexy lingerie to the front grille, condoms to the antenna, and written "Dirty Old Man" on my side of the car. Their artwork eventually saved us a speeding ticket in Oregon. We were doing 50 MPH in a 35 MPH zone and got pulled over. But when the cop came to the window he said, "Slow it down a little bit, lovebirds," and let us go.

When I first asked Dawn to marry me, I had hoped that the real estate market would turn around enough to take her on a dream trip for our honeymoon–maybe Hawaii or Tahiti. As 2010 went on and the sales didn't materialize, I realized that was a pipe dream. At one point, I told Dawn our honeymoon might be spent at the Motel 6 in Tukwila. She said she didn't care. You've gotta love an understanding woman.

Several months before the wedding, the Weibles came through for us again. They told me they had a timeshare and wanted to let us use it as a wedding present. Thanks to them, our honeymoon was saved. The way their timeshare worked, we didn't have to choose just one place to stay—we could split our nights up however we wanted. Jerry, Lynn and I had a wonderful time figuring out how we would spend their points. We decided on a tour of California that included stops in Clear Lake, Oceanside and Anaheim.

By the time we got on our way, it was past 9 pm. We still needed to stop in Chehalis so we could change out of our wedding finery and back into civilian clothes. I loved wearing my tuxedo at the wedding, but when I changed into my Beatles T-shirt, jeans, and tennis shoes, I felt more like myself.

We spent our first day as husband and wife driving down the Oregon Coast on Highway 101. It was a lovely blue-sky-and-sunshine day, with the ocean as our constant companion. We listened to music, audio books, and the sound of breaking waves. Mostly we decompressed after a stressful few weeks.

When we pulled into Oceanside three days later, it felt like we were coming home even though neither one of us had ever been there before. Our original plan was to use Oceanside as a base of operations for forays into San Diego, just a short drive to the south. As soon as we wandered into Oceanside, we forgot all about San Diego. We were so charmed by the city, we never wanted to leave.

Oceanside has a terrific sandy beach, and even though it was late October, the water was warm enough to swim in. Mrs. Inmon and I went swimming everyday alongside the pier. We might as well have been teenagers again. We swam and wrestled and practiced body surfing. It occurred to me that our honeymoon in 2010 wasn't much different from the same honeymoon we would have had if we had gotten married in 1979.

Standing in the warm water, laughing and hopelessly in love, I knew life couldn't ever get any better.

And yet it does. Every day.

Afterword –
Whatever's Written In Your Heart

This book is the story of finding your true love, losing her, and being lucky enough to find her again. It's also about perspective. *Perspective is everything.* If Dawn and I had been able to marry in 1979, we would still be married. We would be happy and have a lifetime of memories to go with our love. But we wouldn't have the gift of perspective we now enjoy. I don't know if we would have the same appreciation for each other without the gift of knowing what our lives would be like without each other.

In the end, our life is the sum of the choices we make, large and small, every day.

Acknowledgments

I received an education while writing this book. I have been lucky to find so many helpful, intelligent, insightful people, both professionally and personally. Thanking them here seems like a pale compensation for all they've given me, but it is what I have to give. I feel a great depth and sincerity of appreciation for:

Chris Guthrie, Open Book Editors – When I first met Chris, I had a story in search of a book. Through his consistent, thoughtful efforts, he helped me break many of the bad writing habits I started with (those remaining are my fault, not his) and helped me shape this book in more ways than I can count.

J.K. Kelly – I hired J.K. to proofread the manuscript and be the final set of eyes before publication. He caught all my errant commas and misplaced italics, but he did much more for me as well. He turned the dry art of proofing into further lessons in writing that I will carry with me into my next book and beyond.

Linda Boulanger, Tell~Tale Book Covers – Linda was infinitely patient and always full of fun creative ideas for the way the book looks. It was her idea to show the two couples in silhouette on the front and back cover that so perfectly captures the innocent essence of the story. She also formatted the book to look great whether you're holding pages in your hand or it is displayed on your e-reader.

Weeb Heinrich, WritingRaw.com – If Weeb hadn't started WritingRaw.com and published the earliest drafts, I don't know how my story would have made it into Dawn's hands. Weeb was supportive and encouraging at a time I needed it most.

It took me five and a half years to write this book. At various stages I had beta readers who looked the manuscript over and offered input and criticism. For the first three of those years, my sister Terri, was the only person who knew I was writing it, and she was my constant conspirator. Later, my most-helpful readers were Karen Lichtenwalter, Bob Mckean, Sherry Eddy, Alice Guenther, Jeff Hunter, Sharil Simmons, Tim Hudson, Lois Walker and Heather Brush. I owe them all a debt of gratitude.

I would also like to thank the teachers of Mossyrock High School, especially Dayton Grimes, Dennis Merz, Lynn Warfield and Jim Bartee. They taught me so much.

Finally and most importantly, I'd like to thank the love of my life, Dawn Adele Inmon, and our five gorgeous daughters: Desi, Connie, Samy, Dani and Brina. I love you all.